SENSORY
INTELLIGENCE

SENSORY INTELLIGENCE

why it matters more than IQ and EQ

Annemarie Lombard

METZ PRESS

SENSORY
INTELLIGENCE

why it matters more than IQ and EQ

Annemarie Lombard

METZ PRESS ■■

Published by Metz Press
1 Cameronians Avenue
Welgemoed, 7530, South Africa

First published in 2007
Second printing 2011
Copyright © Metz Press 2007, 2011
Text copyright © Annemarie Lombard
Illustrations copyright © Annemarie Lombard

SENSORY INTELLIGENCE ™ is a trademark of Annemarie Lombard.
www.sensoryintelligence.co.za

The checklists and profiling tools in this book are for personal use only. Under no circumstances are they to be used for commercial gain without the written permission of the copyright holders.

Publisher & editor	Wilsia Metz
Design & layout	Liezl Maree
Illustrations	Liezl Maree
Index	Liezl Maree
Printing & binding	Paarl Media, 15 Jan van Riebeeck Drive, Paarl
ISBN	978-1-919992-64-8

Foreword

The idea that our sensory experiences are an integral part of our human experience is becoming more apparent every day. Marketing specialists use many sensory references to tap our interest in their products. Designers consider the impact of environmental features on our sensory experiences in spaces they create. Retailers move their products around to attract our senses and our interest in their goods. Yet sensory experiences are so much part our everyday experiences that we can miss the impact of sensation on our mood and ultimately our ability to enjoy our lives.

Annemarie Lombard is bridging the gap between what professionals and researchers know about sensation and what the public would benefit from knowing. She translates ideas from research into practical ideas for enhancing our everyday experiences. When parents, partners, friends and co-workers understand each other and why they are reacting the way they do, it will be easier to make adjustments in spaces, plans and interactions.

Winnie Dunn (PhD OTR FOATA)
Professor & Chair
Department of Occupational Therapy Education
University of Kansas Medical Center

I was very fortunate to have been involved in a personal sensory profiling exercise with Annemarie as she was deepening her research work and the result of that profiling was quite astounding. The accuracy of the reporting, which was based on a self administered questionnaire, was extremely high in relation to the way I behave and the way others see me. I have been involved in major corporations all my working life where I have had access to numerous personality profiling tools designed to help build a deeper understanding of how we behave and how we react in specific situations. What I found astounding about the work that Annemarie has developed is it identifies behaviour stemming from a deeply rooted place way down in our DNA, expressed through how our body interacts with the world through our senses. The fact that I love loads of a complex stimuli, music, noise, light, movement etc. was clearly indicated. It highlighted in a very real way how I interact with my surroundings and that I was a very good fit for my current environment which involves high levels of travel, public interaction, movement and new environments. My profile indicated clearly that I thrive on this and have a high sensory threshold and actually seek out sensory stimulation. The profiling and diagnostics afterwards also indicated that I need to find strategies to enforce mini breaks in this stimulus to avoid any potential overload. (Read all about it in this book!) It has brought a deeper, more meaningful understanding of how I see myself and how I interact with not only those around me, but with the environment where I operate and live.

Many of us grew up in the era of IQ testing at school, university and especially in the workplace and it had its obvious uses but was, as we now know, a relatively blunt tool. Then we were exposed to EQ or Emotional Intelligence and all the work that Daniel Goleman pioneered to look at how we interact as people through our behaviours. As we know, this has had a massive impact on the way that all groupings of people, from couples to huge organs of state, have and are behaving today.

The work that Annemarie has developed, Sensory Intelligence™, in my opinion has struck on what is the highest order of understanding ourselves as this centres on the way our bodies, through our senses, react to the mass of stimuli around us, not just human stimuli but, as importantly, environmental stimuli.

This deeper understanding of ourselves and how we react to different environments has enormous potential individually as we strive and thrive to be more effective in our lives. This will also be an extremely valuable and important application in team effectiveness, management and leadership behaviour, corporate culture and effectiveness in organizations across the world as we strive to understand, empower and harness the true diversity that exists within.

David Crow
Managing Director
British American Tobacco South Africa

Contents

(*Pseudo names are used in all case studies.)

Introduction

His eyes are wide open, his pupils dilated. He is nervously looking from side to side. I can see he is agitated, moving around on the spot. For a moment I am surprised. What is happening? Why is he acting like this? I can see no real threat in our immediate vicinity. At then it hit me: he is in a grocery shop, squeezed between the isle and two women, one pushing her trolley up against him and the other reaching over him for the cereal box on the shelf behind him. She touched him while doing so, further exacerbating his anxiety. He is clenching the handle of the shopping trolley and our little two-year-old boy sitting in the front, sensing his dad's anxiety, starts to cry. His anxiety at being closed in is now aggravated by the shrill screams of a young child. I make the connection and move in to the rescue. I push aside the shopping trolley to create an escape route. He gives a huge sigh of relief when passing me hurriedly to get out of the corner created very unconsciously by two other shoppers.

This is an excellent example of an automatic fear response evoked in a person by the casual touch of two strangers, while being trapped in a confined space. What for me would pass without the slightest response or reaction, triggered severe discomfort and anxiety in my husband. We tend to think that everyone senses and experiences the world in exactly the same way. But our senses are unique and make each of us different in the way we experience normal day-to-day input from our surroundings. Learning to see the world through the eyes of my sensory sensitive husband has been an interesting and enriching journey. It has helped me look at life differently, encouraging me to make a bigger effort to notice small details, and to stop judging others. A few years back our shopping-centre experience would probably have left me feeling merely irritated by his 'irrational' response. Now I know better.

I have worked with children for many years using sensory integration therapy. By facilitating their development of new skills I helped them integrate their senses in order to improve their interaction, learning and behaviour. But when I started looking at the sensory processing of adults, I discovered a whole new world. Whereas with children I had to trust my clinical observations, testing and reasoning to try to figure out what was going on, the situation is quite different with adults. Every person who has allowed me to join his or her sensory journey has given me tremendous insight into the fact that each person's experience the world through his or her senses is unique and different.

Some of us (like me) crave sensory input. We thrive in a busy, active environment where a lot is going on or many people are involved. We have so-called high thresholds. The brain experiences these inputs as enjoyable and can tolerate multiple sensory input at any given time.

Others, however, do not enjoy a busy, noisy environment and crave the quiet, order and tranquillity that life so often withholds from us. They have so-called low thresholds and quickly feeling overwhelmed and irritated by too much going on around them. They would much rather stay at home and watch a movie on TV, read a book, or just spend some quiet time alone than go out clubbing or having dinner in a busy restaurant.

Now, if we further explore how people with different thresholds relate to each other at home and at work, it becomes a fascinating dynamic to suddenly understand your spouse, child, colleague or employer. Low threshold versus high threshold individuals operate in completely opposite ways. They have different needs; they often approach tasks differently and where there is diversity, there is bound to be conflict. Understanding family and work dynamics from this almost primitive, sensory level has been an 'aha' experience for so many people that I stopped counting long ago.

This book explores the concept of sensory intelligence. It is strongly rooted in the sensory integration theory developed in the 1960s and mostly applied to children with developmental or learning difficulties. But the intricate process of processing and modulating the senses in order to produce correct behaviours and responses remains part of us in our adult environment too. In this book I will explain how we are different with regard to thresholds and how we respond to the environment on a very subliminal, yet primitive level. Even an elementary understanding of sensory intelligence will shed new light on your likes, dislikes, oddities, behaviours and irritations.

Sensory thresholds are part of our genetic make-up, but an insight into and awareness of our sensory needs and preferences can lead us to making the necessary changes in our surroundings. This will help you cope with life more easily, more effectively and give you greater understanding within your relationships, both at home and at work. Your sensory preferences are part of who you are. There is no right or wrong; it is simply how you are wired.

I hope this book will facilitate much discussion, dialogue and further research into this powerful but underestimated field. I also hope and pray that it will open the eyes and ears of many to see and hear and experience how special and unique we have been created.

Your senses are your gateway to your world. Use them well!

To Eugene, my husband
Thank you for your love, support, understanding and keeping my
feet on the ground. This would not have been possible without you.

CHAPTER 1

Reconnecting with the senses – your environment from a sensory perspective

Most of us are quite unaware of the effect of our senses when we are trying to make sense of our environment. But the old saying, 'stop and smell the roses' is quite significant when you are considering where you are and what you are experiencing. The senses are the gateway through which information from the outside world is processed and relayed to our brains.

Your seven senses

We access the world around us through seven senses. These are the five 'visible' senses we all know: sight, hearing, smell, taste and touch. But we also have two 'hidden' senses that relate to movement. These are the vestibular sense – sophisticated sense organs in the inner ear that tell us when our bodies are displaced, and help to orient movement for us – and the proprioceptive sense – feedback from muscle movement and joint position. The proprioceptive sense is sometimes also referred to as the 'body sense'. We only explore those parts of the sensory system we can physically identify in the body's anatomy and make up and the function of which we can pinpoint. Therefore, the sense of intuition (although I believe we do have it) is not explored.

At any given time the brain is flooded with sensory information. The brain is a wonderful, yet complicated and advanced piece of equipment we all have, although we don't always use it particularly well. The brain filters, organizes and translates messages from a massive amount of information through the senses and helps us to focus on the important stuff while deciding what is unimportant. This is necessary as it would be virtually impossible for us to attend to all the information the brain is receiving at any given time. While hearing and seeing things, the brain is also picking up on smell, touch, body position, movement and information from the internal organs. The world we experience is basically a construct that is built from all the sensory information the brain is given. The brain has to continuously edit and prune what it is receiving through the senses. Only what the brain regards as relevant and important is forwarded for action, the rest merely subsides and gets extinguished along the way. And this happens on a primitive, subconscious level.

When was the last time you gave your senses special time and attention? I want you to do it now to experience their power. Take time to orient yourself in your present environment.

 ## SIGHT – THE VISUAL SENSE

What do you *see?* The sense organ for 'seeing' is located in the retina of the eye. It is the most advanced and enormously complex of all the senses. We use it constantly when awake to access the world around us. We recognize the world around us – objects, faces, people – through looking, and the brain forms the 'picture' of what we see.

The brain and the visual sense

The brain gives more of its territory to vision than to any other sense. Light passes through the cornea in the eye (the transparent outer coating), is focused by the lens and then strikes the retina, a three-layered blanket of neurons that covers the entire back surface of the eye-ball. The brain handles the complex process of turning this into an image. The receptors for picking up information for the visual system are located in the retina which contains approximately 120 million rods and 6 million cones. The cones are responsible for colour vision and visual perception in normal or bright light. The rods are more sensitive to low levels of light and provide us with vision when it is dark. Animals, for instance, have far more rods than cones. They can't really see colours, but their night vision is far more advanced than ours.

The intricate brain journey begins where light information is converted into electrical signals carried by special nerves in the brain. The brain maps out colour, intensity, what the eye is seeing, where it is located, the direction, speed and other judgements that the everyday personal computer could just dream of doing. This intricate information is then transferred to a primitive part of the brain which controls our eye movements and reflexes and other information sent to the cortex, the 'CEO' of the brain. These are the top lobes of the brain, separated into a left and right side, called the left and right hemisphere. The cortex hosts millions of 'hard drives' for an almost infinite amount of possible information. Researchers have located thirty-two distinct visual areas in each hemisphere of the brain – an astonishing 64 possible places where visual information can go. This is a complex process between the environment, the eye and the brain so that we can see and connect with the environment. We also have loads of memory stored based on visual information which is accessed continuously while we are trying to see the world around us.

The visual sense in real life

Where and how is seeing important in everyday life? We base a huge amount of our connection to life based on what we see. Personal communication is known to be more powerful when eye contact is made; you have to look at, and see the person you are talking to. The list is endless, but these are some of the most important functions of the visual sense:

- Communicating
- Reading
- Driving
- Watching TV or movies
- Computer usage
- Learning.

Some interesting questions:

1. *Why does working in natural light seem to make people more productive than when working under fluorescent lights?*
2. *Have you ever considered the reason behind your choice of screen saver on your personal computer?*
3. *Why does clutter irritate you? Does it?*
4. *Why are you bothered by moving images on TV, making you feel slightly nauseous? Or when driving, do the telephone poles flicking past make you feel dizzy and disorientated?*

And some of the answers:
1. It is well known through research that natural light has a 'softer' and gentler effect on the eyes, reducing fatigue and making people work better for longer.
2. The choice of screen saver in particular can be based on your individual threshold. When we have a low threshold and tend to be distracted by visual information we prefer a blank screen saver which does not distract us. However, when we have high thresholds and thrive on loads of visual information, we prefer moving, illusionary screen savers, 'feeding' the eye

and brain with more information. Hopefully your screen saver is the right match to your threshold.

3. Clutter would potentially irritate the person with low visual thresholds who gets distracted by visual information quickly. It's as if the brain just attends to too much of what is seen, without filtering out any useless information. Neatness and order would be vital for you to maintain a sense of control and be able to work without snapping at your colleague or boss … which might be a career-limiting reaction. How would you explain to your boss that your response was due to sensory overload in the visual sense?

4. The visual and movement systems work together intimately. When there is a low tolerance of movement and seeing, the brain receives conflicting messages when seeing moving images and is thrown off balance. Fortunately, although you may find it nauseating, the brain has a built-in protective system, called the autonomic nervous system. High-alert states occur when conflicting messages reach the brain, and send instant messages to the gut, heart and organs. That's part of the so-called 'stress response' where the brain-body connections increase the fancy footwork done by the brain to protect us from harm. Usually it passes when the conflicting messages are removed or the brain eventually 'gets used to it'. This process is called habituation.

Next time you look at the world around you, the good, the bad and the ugly, acknowledge that your brain is working through an intricate process of taking in information from the environment and 'showing' you what it is. It is the first line of connection to your environment.

How do we rest the visual system?

Sensory overload is a phenomenon that most of us are exposed to on a daily basis. We live in a world that constantly bombards us with sensory input. If you want your brain and systems to work optimally, you have to let them rest.

- Close your eyes
- Practise visualization techniques
- Close your eyes and dream
- Watch fish moving in a fish tank – visit your local aquarium
- Switch on your lava lamp, look at it and relax
- The important thing is, *TAKE FIVE, TAKE A BREAK.*

HEARING – THE AUDITORY SENSE

What do you *hear*? Hearing happens when our ears pick up vibrations or noise in our environment that are transferred to the brain via nerves for identification. We live in a noise-polluted world. Especially if you live in a city, it is very difficult to find total quiet, unless you are prepared to get up at 4 am to spend some time enjoying the blissful peace of hearing nothing and nobody – and even that is no guarantee! Needless to say, getting enough sleep might then be another hurdle. Like seeing, the sense of hearing helps us access the environment in a primary way.

The brain and the auditory sense

Hearing begins in the ear when sound waves are translated into electrical signals to be sent through the auditory 'wires', first to the primitive parts of the brain and then to the 'CEO' in the auditory cortex. Sound is actually perceived by the brain as vibrations differing in frequency and quality and based on these variables being transferred into signals. The inner part of the ear is filled with fluid, the outer two parts with air. It is inside the inner fluid-filled area, inside the cochlea (the inner hearing organ), where the vibration is translated into electrical signals. These are then transferred through various lower brain structures such as the thalamus (grand central station) and brain stem (connections for survival, fight/flight/fright, and attention) before reaching the 'CEO' which gives them meaning. There are two tiny muscles in the middle ear that start to modulate the sounds reaching the cochlea. It is possibly in these lower or primitive brain connections where the under- or over-response to sound is generated.

The auditory sense in real life

Our ears are switched on 24/7. This makes the sense of hearing a very difficult one to rest. Many of my clients complain about noise levels in current society. It is as if we simply cannot find anywhere quiet anymore. Our ears are vital in orienting us to our world through noise and sounds. Hearing aids our communication processes, helps us to absorb information and learn, and also points out potential dangers. If you hear footsteps behind you when walking down a dark alley at night (don't try this at home) it will most certainly send messages to the brain about potential danger. Any life or work environment is filled with noise, some very necessary in respect of our task at hand, but, a huge amount is background noise. And that's where it gets tricky ... how much background noise can you cope with? The function of hearing in every day life includes:

- Communication with others
- Talking on the phone
- Music
- Listening to instructions
- Radio, TV
- Attending workshops/seminars/classes.

1. *Why do some people get highly upset and frustrated by the popcorn brigade in the movies, when others are completely oblivious to them?*
2. *Why is the fight between those wanting to have the radio on and those wanting it off creating havoc at the office. And how do we solve this problem?*
3. *Why does music have such a calming effect on some people?*
4. *How come some of us can easily talk on a cellphone while driving while others become disoriented if they do that?*

And some of the answers

1. It's a matter of threshold! The popcorn brigade are chewing and making lots of lip and mouth noises, while scratching like hens in their huge packets. The low threshold individual sitting four rows down hears every sound and cannot filter it out, cannot hear what's going on in the movie and becomes frustrated. The high threshold person, on the other hand, possibly even sitting much closer to the muncher, manages to filter out this background noise without even realizing it. No problem!

2. Another threshold scenario: low threshold individuals often struggle to work with background noise and would prefer the radio off in order for them to focus better on the task at hand. However, the high threshold folks enjoy sound and their brains are actually stimulated by it. They work better with the radio on. The solution? It's often a tricky one. Explain thresholds so that staff will have insight into and understand each other's needs. Keep the two extremes as far apart as possible. Radio's on in the morning (your brain usually copes better with information in the morning because of the rest you had during the night) and radio off in the afternoon (sensory input is accumulative, hence a decreasing ability to cope with sensory overload by the end of the day) is one of the solutions.

3. Music has varying healing, stimulating and organizing effects on the brain. Since each individual's brain is unique in its particular way of transporting information, it explains the variation in using music for calming, learning or therapeutic effects. Studies over the years have clearly noted the positive effect of music on the brain.

4. Again, the answer lies in the process of transferring and filtering of sound information that is unique to each of us. Some brains take a lot of energy to perform a particular hearing task, such as talking on the phone. When combining that with a different task like driving your car (movement and planning task), it may make you feel unsure and yes, in some cases disoriented. If this applies to you, don't talk and drive! (It's against the law anyway!)

How do we rest the auditory system?

Auditory overload is a very real and known occurrence in everyday life. We envy those fortunate enough to be working in a quiet, outdoor kind of an environment. The farmer tending his vineyards in the Hex River valley, the fieldworker in the Amazon jungle, the deep-sea diver, and so on. Many of us are trapped in cities and city life with its accompanying noise and more noise. Try the following:

- Listen to calming music
- Put on your headphones, and keep the volume down … you don't want to damage your ears with excessive, loud and high pitched sound
- Move to a quiet space to reduce noise
- If all else fails, use ear plugs
- The important thing is, *TAKE FIVE, TAKE A BREAK.*

TOUCH – THE TACTILE SENSE

What do you *feel?* The sense of touch is located in the skin and physically connects us to the world. It is the sensory system with the widest receptor base: you have skin from the top of your head right down to the soles of your feet. It is also the sensory system which develops first and plays a major role in early development in children. We all know how important and vital the sense of touch is for bonding with a small baby. Although being vital at birth, the sense of touch keeps on developing and remains a key component throughout life in our physical interaction with other people. It is our most powerful and intimate form of communication.

The brain and the tactile sense

Touch is an essential system in terms of survival, bonding, protection, and life and death situations. The basic sensations of touch, temperature and pain all begin in the skin in different specialized receptors for each sensation, each with a specialized pathway to the brain. Sensations of pain and temperature are carried primarily by the protective pathway. This is vital for switching on the 'alarm' systems of the brain as we often respond to pain and/or temperature in a protective manner. When touching a hot plate, you will withdraw your hand instinctively based on the processing of this information via the protective pathway. Light touch and deep pressure together with proprioception (the body sense) are carried via the discriminative pathway in order to help us to determine the qualities of what it is we are feeling through touch. The discriminative pathway is also at work when you put your hand in your pocket and hold and recognize a R5 coin as opposed to a R1 coin. We have more receptors in our hands and mouths as these areas are particularly important tools of touch discrimination.

The sense of touch in real life

Being connected to your tactile system can open a new world to you. Apart from how you communicate with others, your personal space and comfort being in groups can be determined by your sense of and threshold of touch. Daily tasks such as dressing, eating, bathing and grooming are filled with touch experiences.

Some interesting questions:

1. *Why do some of us hate being dirty, and recoil in total 'fear' when approached by a two-year old at a birthday party whose hands, face and feet are just about covered in chocolate cake icing?*
2. *Are you one of those people who will refuse to enter a lift when it is about two-thirds full? And if you enter on the second floor and by the sixth floor your lift neighbours are squeezing you from all sides, would you step out and take the stairs to the 15th floor?*
3. *Do you hate being touched or hugged by other people, especially those you don't know well, and being kissed by a man with a one-day-old beard?*
4. *Does a surprise picnic arranged by your loved one on a beautiful beach with a gentle breeze turn your mood into agitation rather than joy and serenity, with you snapping at him or her for offering you a glass of champagne because there is sand on the rim of the glass?*

And some of the answers

1. It's a matter of threshold. People with low touch thresholds (remember it's skin all over) hate being dirty or being touched by someone who is dirty, never mind how innocent and full of good intentions that two-year old might be. Dirt, especially wet dirt, on the skin switches on the 'alarm system' of the brain and that particular feeling is experienced as extremely uncomfortable and yes, in some cases, even painful.
2. When you are in a full lift surrounded by others your touch system is being triggered continuously. The touch system facilitates your personal space and when invaded too closely this in turn again triggers the alarm system. I often find that individuals with low touch thresholds will stand right at the back of the lift. At least if they can see (and 'scan' for protection) they can anticipate their response more easily. Needless to say, they are much fitter than the high threshold group. Having to revert to stairs a number of times a day will do wonders for anyone's aerobic endurance!
3. People with low touch thresholds are just not your all-time huggers or kissers. They simply do not like that intimate contact with others. They normally

are comfortable with intimate contact with their loved ones. When on the receiving end of a low threshold non-hugger we can feel rejected. Relax, they do love you, but don't show it in a physical way. Those with high touch thresholds enjoy touching, hugging and kissing others, even those they don't know particularly well ... careful ... it may cause trouble in the wrong environment. The bottom line is, it's a matter of personal space and your sense of personal space is often dependent on your touch threshold.

4. Beach, wind, sand ... the worst combination imaginable for someone with a low touch threshold. Having to sit on the beach is just not fun. You definitely want a blanket with no holes; grandma's crochet one won't do it, so use the brand new picnic version which is sand and wet proof on one side. You first have to walk over the sand with it sticking to your toes or seeping through your shoes. You can feel every single grain, and it chafes, and hurts, and sets the brain's alarm system to work. Then you have to manoeuvre that picnic basket, the food and wine without connecting with a single grain of sand and that's virtually impossible. To crown it all, the wind that blows brings moving air and extra sand with it. You will just not enjoy it, and then to be offered champagne in a glass with sand on the rim is just the pits. If you cannot do it the 'de luxe' way: a table with white table cloth with those cute little weights holding it tightly in place, a real plate with your food, real glass without sand, a waiter serving you (from a sand-free, wind-free base) and, of course, an absolutely wind free, quiet evening, opt for a restaurant or a fancy dinner for two at home. (I guess Shirley Valentine would agree).

How do we rest the tactile system?

Sensory overload in the touch system results from being exposed to too many people, too many textures, and too many touches for too long. I once attended a weekend conference where the speaker was wearing a polo neck top. From about ten that morning she started to pull away that polo neck from her body, I could see her irritation increasing. I was sure she was going to change her top during lunch time. But not realising that this was one of the reasons for her sensory overload and resulting drop in focus, she continued wearing the top the whole day with increasing signs of irritability and distraction ... and it was not a pleasant experience for her nor for anyone attending her presentation. Don't try to hang in there – for your own and others' sake! Rather try the following:

- Remove a touch irritation, whether it is a sock with a funny seam, a label, a scratchy blouse, or a polo neck
- You may sometimes want to remove your partner ... it is not recommended, but make sure you have quiet time alone
- A deep massage

- A heavy quilt or blanket
- A big bear hug, not a light kiss
- The important thing is, *TAKE FIVE, TAKE A BREAK.*

SMELL AND TASTE – THE CHEMICAL SENSES

What do you *smell?* What do you *taste?* Smell and taste are the chemical senses reacting to specific molecules in the environment. These are primitive senses: all animals (even single cell organisms) have distinguished smell and taste abilities, often using them for basic survival. The senses of smell and taste are known through human evolution to be crucial for survival. Possibly because these are the most primitive senses involving fewer dedicated brain regions, we find that fewer people are sensitive to smell and taste. There are also fewer sources of confusion and noise, and it is physically easier to adapt to noxious smells and tastes.

The brain and the senses of smell and taste

The smell pathway starts with the response of a smell molecule via the olfactory (smell) bulb in the nose. We have thousands of different chemical detectors in our nose and research shows that the human nose can detect as many as 10 000 odours. After receiving information via the nose, the smell pathway in the brain is short and direct. An important aspect of the sense of smell is that it could be called the 'favourite sense' of the brain, in a manner of speaking. Messages from all other sensory systems have to pass via the thalamus (grand central station in the brain) but smell has a direct pathway, or one could say a 'hotline', to the limbic system. This system is important for emotion and memory and often referred to as the emotional brain. Smells get preference in being sent to the limbic system and then to the cortex which identifies the type of smell in the brain. This accounts for the strong response we have towards a noxious smell and the memory it often accompanies. For this reason also is smell quite potent, as it does not have that additional filter in the thalamus. When something stinks, it really STINKS with a capital S, and makes people run off. The emotional response (from the limbic system) is clear, immediate and profound.

The other primitive sense, taste, accounts for 2 000 to 5 000 taste buds in and around the mouth, detecting taste in four basic categories – sweet, salty, bitter and sour. Full flavour appreciation comes from close interaction between smell and taste. Have you ever tried drinking castor oil while pinching your nose tight and keeping it fully closed? You do not taste the castor oil until you let go of your nose … then the taste hits you … Yaaach! Taste information is carried further via the lower structures in the brain to the cortex for recognition and identification.

An interesting fact about the smell and taste systems is that they regenerate new cells – over a period of 10 days for taste and 30 days for smell. This is necessary because the receptors of these systems are exposed to the environment – hot and cold liquids, spices – and also bombarded by bacteria and dirt, and constantly at risk of drying out. Thank goodness for the wonderful chemistry of the brain that makes new receptor cells for smell and taste all the time.

Temperature also has an effect on taste receptors. If your taste buds are exposed to very cold temperatures, the sense of taste is greatly reduced.

The senses of smell and taste in real life

Our enjoyment or not of food is the most important result of the workings of smell and taste. We rely heavily on these senses to appreciate food. The sense of smell also affects our interaction with others around us. When the smell sense is bombarded with pleasant input, we respond positively to others within the environment. However, when bombarded with a noxious odour, a negative emotional response will be elicited. I recently had a conversation with a human resource manager who interviewed an applicant for a position at their company. During the interview she was so offended by this applicant's body odour that she just could not be convinced to recommend him for the position, despite his qualifications. Yet the other exco members present during the interview seemed oblivious to the smell.

Some interesting questions:

1. *Why do some of us enjoy spicy, hot foods and others are quite put off?*
2. *Why do we have certain memories strongly connected to certain smells?*
3. *Why is aromatherapy a successful method of de-stressing?*
4. *Are flowers and/or perfume always the right gift for that woman you want to impress?*

And some of the answers
1. Again, it's a matter of threshold. Low threshold people prefer known, familiar and often bland foods. I see it over and over in my case studies. On the other hand, people with a high threshold in their taste and smell systems are often those who prefer and enjoy hot, flavourful and spicy foods.
2. Memories often have strong smell associations owing to the direct link between the smell pathway in the brain and the limbic system (the emotional and memory brain). My grandfather had a farm in Namaqualand and whenever I smell Namaqualand daisies it brings back nostalgic memories of

my childhood experiences on the farm. Based on your previous experience, the smell would elicit a positive or a negative reaction.

3. Research clearly shows the positive effect of aromatherapy. The olfactory nerves transmit signals that go to the limbic system and the result is that certain smells calm us, others stimulate us, and yet others help us sleep. Since your brain and sensory system are unique, you will have to experience and explore certain aromas to find the right ones for you. But generally there are groups of aromas that calm versus other groups that stimulate us.

4. Flowers and perfume are perfect gifts for women with normal to high thresholds. Handing your low-threshold girlfriend a bunch of strong smelling lilies which makes her sneeze and gives her a headache in her small apartment, may not be good for the relationship. The same goes for perfume. Although perfume is a very personal thing, some people just cannot tolerate the smell of perfume owing to low threshold for smell. I know of many clients who never wear perfume and hate being close to others who do. Perfume is a chemical with a strong smell and for this reason we also recommend to new mothers not to wear perfume during the first few months of their baby's life. It might easily lead to sensory overload in a little baby, resulting in fussing and/or uncontrolled crying.

How do we rest the smell and taste systems?

Fortunately, as mentioned before, sensory overload in these systems is not that prevalent. When there is overload, however, it is quite difficult to address owing to the short link in the brain. You cannot bypass that link with something else; it is a matter of removing or avoiding the sensory input as much as possible.

- Avoid areas or people with pungent or strong smells
- Find and create the smell that suits your system
- Aromatherapy (with smells that work for you)
- Use air fresheners (with an inoffensive or neutral smell)
- Open windows and/or doors to air closed-in areas
- Eat the foods that you enjoy; be daring and adventurous with foods if you have a high threshold and stick to the known ones if you have a low threshold. It's okay; there are more important things to life than pushing the limits with food
- The important thing is, *TAKE FIVE, TAKE A BREAK.*

MOVEMENT – THE VESTIBULAR AND PROPRIOCEPTIVE SENSES

How do you sense *movement?* When referring to the senses the vestibular and proprioceptive senses are often overlooked. But how could we? Movement impulses reach the brain via the vestibular sense, the gravity sense in your inner ear, and the proprioceptive sense – impulses sent when you use a joint and/or muscle. The vestibular system can be seen as the body's GPS (global positioning system) as it tells us where in space we are, based on movement of the head, and gravity processed through the vestibular apparatus in the inner ear. The proprioceptive system can be described as the 'body sense'. As it processes information from the muscles and joints, this system helps you to walk down a flight of stairs, or tip-toe to the bathroom in pitch darkness at night without having to switch on the light. Your proprioception tells you where your feet and body are and how to move to get to the bathroom without knocking over the dressing table. Hopefully there are no kids' toys lying around to stumble over as your proprioceptive system cannot warn you about that – that's the job of the visual system and if you haven't switched on the light ...

We take movement for granted, but it is a highly important and vital part of human behaviour. It's just that as we get older, motor patterns become programmed and natural – we don't need to think about them anymore.

The brain and the senses of movement

The vestibular process in the brain goes something like this: The influence of the pull of gravity or any change in head position starts a chemical reaction via little hair cells in the fluid in the vestibular system in the inner ear being displaced. From here information is sent to the lower parts of the brain via a nerve that shares information coming from our sense of hearing. There are various connections in this area to the muscles of the body to help you maintain your posture when you are sitting in a chair, for instance, or keeping your head upright. Then the vestibular system has connections with your eye muscles, helping keeping them stable so that you can keep looking at something specific, whether you move your head or not. To see how this works, move your head sideways while reading this. Do the letters move around or can you still read everything clearly? The latter should be true.

The proprioceptive process in the brain works as follows: Information coming from receptors in the muscles and joints is sent to various parts of the body and brain in the form of electrical impulses. Some information travels with information from the sense of touch to the brain while the other bits of information are dispersed to produce fluent movement, plan motor actions and sequence bilateral movements. Information from the two systems (the proprioceptors and the vestibular system) is combined and sent to the cortex to make movement conscious.

There are fewer connections in the cortex for movement, which explains why we are not as conscious of our movement than we are of what we see or hear (with the senses of sight and hearing having extensive cortex chambers).

The senses of movement in real life

The brain turns any learnt movement into an unconscious process so that we only need to think about it when learning a new skill. However, researchers have also established a link between movement, learning and emotion. So even though movement is automatic and not one of the obvious senses, it both affects learning and is indicated by mood. Have you noticed the body posture of someone who's depressed? And the body posture of someone ecstatically happy about something? Learning in the brain requires various forms of sequencing. Sequencing of movement kind of paves the way for the brain to learn how to sequence other things. But movement is basic, like breathing. In real life we use the movement senses for:

- Sitting on a chair
- Moving/walking between objects
- Driving your car
- Exercise, running, biking, walking, etc.
- Using an escalator, stairs or a lift
- Finding a new place
- Bending down
- Dancing.

Some interesting questions:

1. *How come some people get such a thrill from amusement parks while others refuse to go? Why are young people in particular drawn to roller-coaster rides and other adrenaline-pumping activities?*
2. *Why do people get sea sick or car sick?*
3. *How come I feel on top of the world after a vigorous run or aerobic exercise?*
4. *Would the senses of movement dictate the type of sport people choose?*

And some of the answers

1. It is (you've guessed it) a matter of threshold. Some of us (excluding me) love going on a roller-coaster ride and have adrenaline and happy hormones pumping for ages thereafter, wanting to go again and again and again. Their brains have high thresholds of movement and can tolerate, excessive amounts of movement while experiencing a positive emotion. Here again

the brain establishes a link between emotion and movement. Others with a low threshold of movement get sick and would vomit on a roller coaster. In this instance the vestibular system is working overtime since the position of the head is changed 360° at high speeds. The autonomic nervous system links are triggered much faster and more intensely in those with a low threshold, therefore the resultant nausea. Research also indicates that younger people have more sensation-seeking traits and that these traits diminish slightly as we get older. This also has something to do with the fact that children and young people are very active and challenge their movement systems more regularly and more intensely than older adults. *I don't want to get side-tracked here, but most recent research shows that children today are far more inactive and that obesity among children has become a far bigger problem than decades ago. So parents, get your children out of the house and move!*

2. Nausea resulting from car sickness or sea sickness occurs when there are mixed messages between the vestibular system, the visual system and the brain, resulting in the autonomic nervous system being triggered. Movement nausea is more prominent among individuals with a low vestibular threshold. Remember, the vestibular system is triggered by movement where there is a change of head position and the visual field and eyes are always involved. People with a low vestibular threshold can have high or normal proprioceptive thresholds. Therefore, movement in general is not necessarily a potential area of discomfort, but only where head positioning is involved.

3. The movement system is connected to the reticular activating system. This system in the brain controls your state of wakefulness and determines whether you are awake, alert or sleepy. When you are physically active your brain's state of alertness is heightened, so you feel alive and on top of the world after exercise. Of course, coupled with this is the release of happy hormones, adding to this nice glow of feeling good. John Ratey in his book *A user's guide to the brain* says: "movement is medicine …". No wonder exercise has become a billion dollar industry. Have you joined yet?

4. Without a doubt our movement thresholds clearly dictate our choice of sport. Those with a low vestibular threshold will not do gymnastics, sailing or rock climbing. Other high adrenaline sports such as abseiling, skydiving, bungee jumping, etc. also place high demands on the vestibular system and will be avoided. Canoeing, biking or running might be the sport of choice for people with a low vestibular threshold as there is very little change in head position, with movement more or less restricted to going forward (see page 85).

How do we rest the movement systems?

Movement overload is not that prevalent either, although nausea related to movement in a car or boat is. There are effective ways of reducing movement-related nausea. The movement system is a very strong self-regulator and often used to calm the other senses when in overload.

- When you feel nauseous or experience motion sickness, look straight ahead. This reduces the conflicting messages received by the brain. Put something in your mouth to suck or chew on
- Smooth, rhythmic movement, like hanging in a hammock, is calming and relaxing
- Get to a quiet spot, find a comfortable position, and be still
- Get some sleep
- The important thing is: *TAKE FIVE, TAKE A BREAK.*

The brain, the core of the senses, in more depth

Although I've given you glimpses of the pathways of each sensory system within the brain, we also need to look at the mix of senses and how it affects the brain as a whole. The brain is extremely complicated and has been described as the most complex system in the universe. I will attempt a greatly simplified explanation to place the sensory systems in perspective. We can never know everything there is to know about the brain which continues to fascinate researchers in many fields.

BRAIN MODULATION IN A NUTSHELL

Let's take a brief look at the general and global way sensory input from the environment is processed in the brain. The important fact to remember is that the brain has hierarchies, like any social system in the world.

The hierarchy

The lowest level is the *brain stem,* also called the primitive brain.

The brain stem is in charge of survival and drives the functions necessary for self-preservation: feeding, fleeing, fighting and reproduction. In the core of the brain stem is the reticular activating system (RAS), the seat for sleep cycles, arousal and attention and therefore consciousness. The RAS extends from the spinal cord to the thalamus, which is the brain's sensory Grand Central Station. All sensory information processed by the brain passes through the thalamus, except sensations of smell.

The *cerebellum* is a structure behind the brain stem acting as the puppeteer of the nervous system. It is responsible for coordinating all our body movements so we can move easily, smoothly, precisely and with good timing.

The next level is the *limbic system,* also called the emotional brain, and is the next station for sensations. The limbic system is the seat of feelings and moods.

It is here, thanks to neurotransmitters and hormones, that we 'feel' and interpret sensations to match emotions. All sensations (except those of smell) pass through the gates of the primitive brain en route to the limbic system. Sharon Heller in her book, *Too loud, too bright, too fast, too tight*, says that sensations and emotions are forever married. The limbic system and the reticular activating system work together to modulate the nervous system.

The third and highest level is the *cortex,* the 'acting CEO' of the nervous system. Our executive functions of thinking, reasoning and doing are generated here. This part of the brain enables you to write, speak, plan, make decisions, do calculations and get you into university. It gives you some control, or willpower, over the primal lower commands.

Communication between the levels

There is a smooth three-way communication process between all these levels.

In a smoothly functioning nervous system the primitive brain sets up the integrity of the entire nervous system. To function well and allow for more complex and specialized information, the cortex CEO must rely on adequate sensory organization and management at the lower, less complex levels. When this happens, the connections between the three parts of the brain work in harmony and effective sensory modulation and integration occur automatically. You spontaneously adjust your actions to signals from the environment, and your senses create curiosity and excitement. Your brain responds by creating the necessary mental set for the activity at hand and your behaviour is efficient, goal-directed, and purposeful.

So how does sensory intelligence (SIQ) relate to intelligence quotient (IQ) and emotional intelligence (EQ)? I believe the answer lies to a degree in how we look at the different processing levels in the brain.

IQ involves the cortex of the brain, the top CEO part, as the vital link for facilitating executive functions of action, reasoning, abstract thinking, etc. This is a major brain component that we utilize to perform at our best.

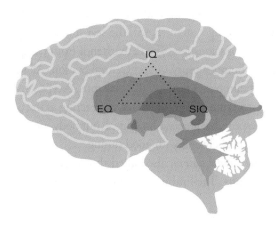

The top executives and CEO cannot function without the people below them supporting their role and vision. The same applies to the human brain. When we look at a diagram of the brain we see that there are numerous structures in the middle and lower parts of the brain playing a vital role in processing sensory information. It is at the primitive lower level of the brain, the brain stem and midbrain that a large part of sensory processing occurs (the section marked SIQ). Of course we tap into the CEO of the brain, that is ultimately our goal, but it is through the lower, primitive structures that we modulate and regulate sensory information for action and performance. Emotional intelligence is mainly seated in the limbic system, hence its indication in the midbrain.

The triangle is an indication of the three-way interaction between these three intelligences. They all affect one another and work in collaboration to optimize brain capacity and function.

NATURE VS NURTURE

How the brain processes information and how much the brain can tolerate based on thresholds are based on two main factors. The first is *nature*. We are born with a certain genetic predisposition to either over- or under-respond to sensations from the environment. Clinical practice clearly demonstrates the fact that sensitive children are often the product of sensitive adults. That explains the power of genes. We are just born a certain way. Research clearly shows traits to be genetically passed on from generation to generation. Therefore, you are born with your threshold. This should already make you feel better. The core neurological threshold we refer to in occupational therapy in sensory integration is genetic predisposition. It is not something you've chosen or become. You are born with it.

But we must also consider the second factor, namely *nurture*. This refers to our upbringing based on environment, culture and role models. Obviously our gene pool weighs heavily, but thresholds are moulded through the way we are brought up. If you were brought up in a small suburban house with five siblings, your tactile thresholds will certainly be higher than someone who grew up on a farm, in a huge homestead, with one sibling. Your system was challenged while you were growing up and your brain just had to habituate, or get used to, all the people and noise around you. A very interesting bit of research quoted by John Ratey in *A user's guide to the brain* also illustrates the impact of culture very clearly. He refers to a study on adults in social settings that counted the number of times people touched each other casually (patting or touching a friend's shoulder). They found that in cafés in France touching between people occurred 200 times in 30 minutes, as opposed to only twice in the United States. So be warned: stay away from France if you have been classified tactile defensive!

Nature and nurture are extensively moulded in individuals, each contributing a great deal to the development of thresholds. Valuable information regarding this will be discussed in the relationship sections (see Chapter 4), among others to caution parents not to deprive their children of sensory stimulation owing to their own low threshold patterns. Have you ever seen a tactile sensitive mother with a dirty child? No, they're squeaky clean from head to toe! But getting dirty is part of growing up and provide important and valuable sensory stimulation opportunities which facilitate a child's development.

DEFENSIVE VERSUS SEEKING SENSORY SYSTEMS

Throughout this book we will explore the two extremes of sensory threshold. On the one end we have people with low thresholds who are sensitive, categorized 'defensive' when sensitivity is extreme. Sensory defensiveness is characterized by averse or defensive reactions to what most people would consider non-irritating sensory stimuli.

A low threshold or low tolerance results in the brain over-reacting or over-responding. It often leads to tension, anxiety, avoidance, stress, anger and even violence. Basic sensations have the potential to put the brain into 'high-alert', which coincides with a stress response.

Degrees of sensory defensiveness can be mild, moderate or severe. The higher the degree of defensiveness, the higher the impact on your quality of life and the resulting stress. Defensiveness can be evident in one or more sensory system. If someone is defensive to auditory stimulation, sounds and noise will potentially overload the brain.

Although largely unrecognized, sensory defensiveness is not uncommon. Studies in the USA showed that 15% of normal adults have a nervous system that is overly sensitive to sensation. They potentially become irritable, distracted as their brains keep going into fight/flight responses. The following adjectives may describe someone who is potentially a sensory defensive person: difficult, picky, perfectionist, anti-social, demanding, fussy, finicky, fastidious. Understanding these behaviours is the key in order to implement appropriate coping strategies.

At the other extreme we have people with high thresholds who tend to under-register what goes on in their environment and can often be sensation seeking. This group of people responds to a 'sensory hunger' based on too little information being processed. Research has found some correlations between sensation-seeking traits and substance abuse patterns.

In my experience, however, it is the low threshold group who seems to have more difficulty coping with life and its stressors and this book will focus mainly on this group. This is heavily based on case studies and in my current exposure I work with far more people with low thresholds than with high thresholds.

However, when we explore relationship dynamics and goodness of fit profiles between individuals it is vital to consider all profiles across the threshold continuum.

SENSORY STIMULATION OF THE BRAIN ACROSS ALL AGES

Have you ever tried to count how many somersaults and cartwheels a five-year old could do in the span of one day? Quite a few, if you can succeed in dragging them away from the computer and the TV. Have you counted how many somersaults and cartwheels most adults do in the span of one day? Not one! I do believe we should, though I guess we may end up in hospital with all sorts of injuries. And don't even mention the looks of utter disbelief in the eyes of bystanders! This is unfortunately or fortunately a fact of life. As we grow older we become less active on a sensory level.

Generally looking at pensioners in retirement homes one might say that they are at a point of being sensory deprived. They don't move, touch, see or hear as much as they used to. Their world becomes smaller, often due to deteriorating health and their sensory input diminishes greatly. Together with less sensory input a sense of worthlessness and depression sets in. An important lesson to learn from this is to stay active and seek sensory stimulation for as long as you can. Your typical sensation seekers are the ones whose stories you read in the newspapers when they do bungee jumps and parachute jumps at the age of 70 and even 80. Well done, keep it up, but please proceed with caution and let safety prevail.

PLASTICITY IN THE HUMAN BRAIN

One other amazing thing about the brain is that contrary to myth and general belief, the brain continues to grow and form certain new cells until the day that you die. Although seriously complex your brain is the best tool you'll ever have! So use it well.

According to the theories of neural plasticity, your brain can be stretched and challenged forever. I know that change is difficult but it is possible. It also confirms the fact that our neurological thresholds, what we can tolerate, can change. If we are in a good space we can usually tolerate more. When stressed, ill or going through major life changes, our thresholds diminish and we feel that we can tolerate even less than usual. The threshold point of a brain is therefore not a specific point but should rather be seen as a shifting band. We rarely have dramatic shifts, but thresholds do move and are based on our current situation and personal predisposition.

Summary of the senses from a scientific perspective

So now you have been introduced to the world around you through the senses. I hope that it has brought you a bit closer to the sensory you and has possibly already explained some weird patterns and/or strange behaviours. In the rest of this book we will explore the process of *sensory modulation* in considerable depth. When referring to sensory modulation I need to take you a step back into where this daily phenomenon fits into the scientific world. Sensory modulation refers to the processing of sensory information from the senses at any given time. The brain is bombarded with sensory information via the seven senses and also through the internal organs. The brain filters this information to help you attend to the important information while ignoring the unimportant information. This process of modulating sensory input is therefore crucial for us to function optimally on a daily basis. It has a huge impact on our productivity, focus, attention, communication and social interactions.

Sensory modulation is a sub-theory of sensory integration, a model of therapeutic intervention developed and pioneered by an American occupational therapist, A. Jean Ayres. Traditionally and originally sensory integration had its development in the neuroscience approach to child development and became the treatment of choice for children with learning and perceptual difficulties. The sensory integration process also has a strong neuroscience basis. In other words, how the brain is structured and functions, supports the theory and application of sensory integration.

Sensory integration remains a specialist field in the occupational therapy profession. Although still mostly centred on child development in South Africa and across the world, the application of this powerful technique is growing rapidly to incorporate individuals across all lifespans, cycles and ages. Clinical experience and the latest research have taken the theory of sensory integration to a new level. Based on child development research, we know this process is crucial between the ages of two and eight for children. However, we now utilize this powerful and unique approach to babies from birth. The same applies to adults. Sensory integration is not solely a paediatric application anymore. Sensory integration is a daily, unique and very necessary process we *all* use in order to make sense of our world.

This book will explore and highlight the sensory modulation process for all of us. We are continuously processing sensory information but everyone does so uniquely. That is why this tool is so useful. Looking at the world through your eyes does not mean this is what the world looks like. Your partner, child, colleague, friend or employee in all likelihood processes information from the environment totally differently from the way you do. This insight and knowledge together with suggested facilitating strategies (your sensory intelligence) will help you understand yourself and the people around you better and lead to improved interaction.

To Winnie Dunn and Erna Blanche, my idols in the field of sensory integration. Thank you for your inspiration and for giving me the knowledge and tools I needed to write this book!

CHAPTER 2

Sensory profiling and assessments

The boxes or so-called comfort zones in which we tend to operate are a definite no-no for me. However, I have to rely on putting people into boxes in order to understand their sensory traits and profiles. The main aim of this chapter is to assist you in trying to determine who you are on a sensory level; trying to determine where you fit in from a sensory profile perspective. Once you have done that, you can use this insight to explore further this dynamic process between you and your home, work and social environments.

Getting ready

While profiling yourself, keep the following in mind:
- There is no right or wrong; your profile is merely a reflection of who you are and you do not need any fixing! It is about understanding a unique and primitive relationship which has great potential to improve your quality of life.
- Your sensory profile is a reflection of the primitive you – meaning it highlights your comfort zone where you'll operate best and most comfortably. We all can and do move out of our comfort zones.
- You might not fit exactly into some quadrants, but you should be able to get a general picture.
- You should complete the profile questions when your life is not in any kind of turmoil. When depressed, ill or going through a difficult time, you might over-score on some questions as your current emotional state can influence your outlook on life extensively.
- This is a subjective method of profiling you from a sensory perspective. In clinical practice, this process is far more extensive with the compilation of background and current information, together with a formal assessment.

- Each profile has a positive and a negative side. Please don't get locked into the negative side. I urge you to identify the positive side of your profile. Learn to understand and live with the negative side of your profile but *please* remember and live through the positive side.
- Your sensory profile is a genetic predisposition; in other words, you should identify traits and when you think back, or ask your mother, you should have shown similar traits as a child or baby. The theory on which my discussion is based, takes genetic make-up moulded through upbringing as point of departure. Your profile should therefore reflect you in general, from a young age. It cannot reflect your state of being for just a part of your life, say, the last few months or years.
- Research does, however, show that your sensory profile tends to shift slightly as you get older. Think about it, the sensory inputs of people in an old age home will generally differ from that of teenagers. Therefore, based on our lifestyle and roles, we do find more sensory sensitive behaviours occurring as we get older. I am speculating that this is purely owing to an under-utilization of our senses. When was the last time you saw granny skateboarding?
- You will determine your sensory profile and traits by completing a behaviour checklist as well as the Sensory Systems Checklist (see page 48). I have developed this tool working with adults since 2002. I based it on a standardized test called the Adult/Adolescent Sensory Profile developed by American occupational therapists, Catana E. Brown and Winnie Dunn, published in 2002. Prior to that Winnie Dunn developed sensory profiles for children and infants respectively. You can access these tools from www.sensoryprofile.com. I felt the need to expand on the sensory profile quadrants and also look at the systems separately, which add depth and further understanding to the profile.
- Having worked with sensory integration for 17 years and having obtained histories and case studies from hundreds of adult clients over the past five years enabled me to expand on the profile. The sensory system checklist will enable you to get a sense of your profile and what to do about it. Insight is an essential part of my intervention process. Understanding yourself from this primitive and sensory perspective will be crucial in choosing strategies to improve on your life. I will also share interesting case studies with you. Do note that all case studies are of true clients, but are shared anonymously and pseudonyms are used to protect their identity.

Understanding sensory terminology

A basic understanding of sensory terminology will ensure that you derive the most benefit from your sensory profiling.

NEUROLOGICAL THRESHOLDS AND SELF-REGULATION

Neurological threshold refers to how much information a particular person's brain needs in order to start firing the response in the nervous system – switching on the brain currents and sending them to the cortex through the lower structures of the brain. The brain, being flooded with millions of sensory inputs at any given time, will determine what is important and respond to it, and what is unimportant, and ignore it. When the brain responds to sensory information it sensitizes to the information and recruits more brain cells in order to send the message through. When the brain ignores sensory information it habituates and no message is transmitted. This balance in the brain helps us to stay focused and attentive in order to act on the sensory information.

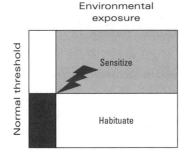

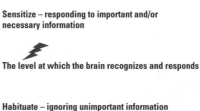

Sensitize – responding to important and/or necessary information

The level at which the brain recognizes and responds

Habituate – ignoring unimportant information

At the one extreme people with a *high neurological threshold* need a lot of information to start the firing process in the brain. Too much habituation takes place in people with high thresholds. Habituation is when the brain recognizes information as familiar or unimportant and ignores that input. Habituation in the brain is crucial in order to block out unnecessary information so that the brain can attend to and focus on relevant information. But the high threshold individual uses too much habituation and the brain under-responds.

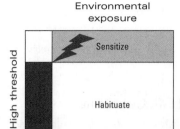

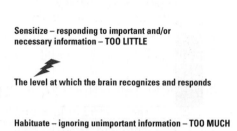

Sensitize – responding to important and/or necessary information – **TOO LITTLE**

The level at which the brain recognizes and responds

Habituate – ignoring unimportant information – **TOO MUCH**

At the other extreme people with *low thresholds* need very little information to start the firing process in the brain. Their brains tend to sensitize too often and intensely. Sensitizing is when the brain recognizes something as novel or potentially dangerous and responds to it. Sensitizing is important in everyday life so that we will attend to what is important. But the low threshold individual uses too much sensitizing and the brain over-responds.

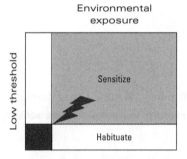

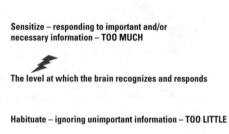

Sensitize – responding to important and/or necessary information – **TOO MUCH**

The level at which the brain recognizes and responds

Habituate – ignoring unimportant information – **TOO LITTLE**

Self-regulation is the other important term in sensory profiling. The brain has a natural tendency to create homeostasis or balance within the brain. When we self-regulate we try to balance out what is potentially difficult for the brain to handle. We all respond differently to sensory input and our responses are based on our neurological thresholds (low, high or normal). Sometimes the brain acts in accordance with the threshold and kind of "goes with the flow". This is a passive response. At other times the brain wants to actively counteract the thresholds and resists or "goes against" the threshold. This is an active response which is recognized by a particular action against the threshold. If we have a high threshold, the brain might potentially feel deprived of sensory input and seek more.

If we have low thresholds, the brain might potentially feel overloaded of sensory input and avoid more. Self-regulation through the senses is an important tool to use for organizing, alerting or calming the brain. This is discussed in detail in Chapters 6 and 7. It is also used to establish a sensory diet – activities you need to build into your daily life to calm, energize or feed your brain.

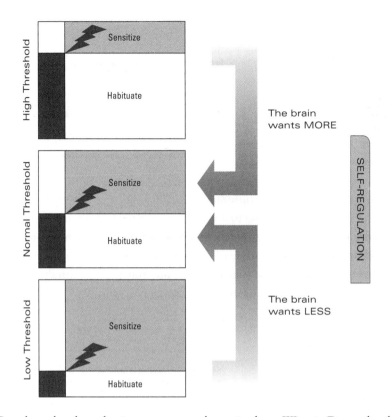

Based on the above brain processes and terminology, Winnie Dunn developed the *model of sensory processing*, which in turn forms the basis of the sensory profile score and results in this book.

Sensory Profile Quadrants

		BEHAVIOURAL RESPONSE / SELF-REGULATION CONTINUUM	
		Passive	Active
NEUROLOGICAL THRESHOLD CONTINUUM	High (Habituation)	**Low Registration**	**Sensation Seeking**
	Low (Sensitization)	**Sensory Sensitivity**	**Sensation Avoiding**

When we start 'labelling' people according to how they respond to sensory input, we use four main sensory profile categories which are:

- *Low registration:* Individuals in this group have high thresholds but respond passively to their thresholds.
- *Sensation seeking:* Individuals in this group also have high thresholds but respond actively to their thresholds.
- *Sensory sensitive:* Individuals in this group have low thresholds but respond passively to their thresholds.
- *Sensation avoiding:* Individuals in this group have low thresholds but respond actively to their thresholds.

To simplify the profile process for the purpose of this book, we will first look at two main categories:

- People with low thresholds – their brains are more in tune with the environment, they notice more information and tend to go into overload more rapidly.
- People with high thresholds – their brains tend to tune out more information; they notice less in the environment and take longer to reach sensory overload.

Looking at responses, namely passive versus active responses, is also important, especially when trying to find ways to self-regulate. At this point passive and active responses are grouped together and the only distinction is between low and high thresholds.

High versus low thresholds

I compiled a list of questions based on documented profile tendencies and my clinical experience which you can use to form an idea of your processing style. Answer yes or no to the following questions and base your answers on how you generally respond. An answer of not applicable should only be used if it is not relevant to your life.

High neurological threshold indicators	YES	NO	N/A
1. Do you enjoy and seek out fast carnival rides that move or spin excessively?			
2. Do you enjoy wearing bright and colourful clothing?			
3. Do you participate or would like to take part in adrenaline sports (skydiving, ocean diving, skiing, surfing, rock climbing, etc.)?			

High neurological threshold indicators	YES	NO	N/A
4. Do you like trying out new restaurants rather than going to familiar ones?			
5. Do you enjoy socializing in big groups of people?			
6. Do you tend to add spices to your food?			
7. Are you adventurous with new foods?			
8. Do you tend to do things on the spur of the moment?			
9. Do you enjoy being close to people who wear perfume or cologne, or enjoy the aroma of scented candles, bath products?			
10. Do you enjoy moving around and are you often "on the go"?			
11. Do you get bored and restless easily?			
12. Do you find it difficult to sit still and concentrate for long periods of time?			
13. Do you like walking barefoot?			
14. Do you usually touch other people while talking to them?			
15. Do you hum, whistle, sing or make other noises while engaged in other activities?			
16. Do you usually do more than one thing at the same time?			
17. Do you cope well with change and often welcome it?			
18. Do you like surprises?			
19. Do you tend to overindulge with food or drink?			
20. Do you sometimes notice scrapes or bruises without remembering how you got them?			

If you have answered 'yes' to 12 or more of the above questions, you may have a high threshold or high tolerance for sensory input. If you respond passively, you tend to under-register the sensory information in your environment and often take longer to register sensations. If you respond actively, you tend to seek out sensory input, creating opportunities to add activity and/or sensations to your environment. Sensation seekers tend to be actively and continuously engaging with their environment; they are energetic, excitable and enjoy busy environments. They may be easily distracted and have difficulty concentrating. They enjoy change and need novel and varied activities to keep them interested.

Low neurological threshold indicators	YES	NO	N/A
1. Do you seem overly sensitive to sounds?			
2. Do you blink at bright lights or seem irritated or fatigued by them?			
3. Do you become distracted by lots of noise?			
4. Do you become motion sick easily (cars, boats, planes)?			
5. Do you avoid fast, spinning carnival rides?			
6. Are you overly sensitive to and aware of odours (perfumes, foods)?			
7. Do clothing textures, labels, socks, turtlenecks, pantyhose, hats, or jewellery bother you?			
8. Do you avoid getting your hands dirty and messy?			
9. Do you strongly dislike light touch from other people and avoid crowds and standing in line?			
10. Do you dislike using creams, perfumes, and/or lotions?			
11. Do you get irritated by people in the movies chewing popcorn? Or whispering and talking to others?			
12. Do you dislike shaving, hair cutting and/or nail clipping/filing?			
13. Do you need a lot of time alone, or enjoy being alone?			
14. Do you have a strong desire for sameness, structure and routine?			
15. Do unexpected events, changes of schedules, or surprises upset and unsettle you?			
16. Do you often feel anxious and/or overwhelmed?			
17. Are you fussy with food? Do you avoid eating trifle? Do you keep your food separately on your plate?			

Low neurological threshold indicators	YES	NO	N/A
18. Do you avoid lifts/elevators preferring to use the stairs?			
19. Do you dislike being hugged or touched, especially from behind?			
20. Do you tend to be controlling as a person?			

If you have answered 'yes' to 12 or more of the above questions, you may have a low threshold or low tolerance for sensory input, you are sensory sensitive and tend to avoid sensations from the environment. If you respond passively, you tend to be sensitive to your sensory environment, over-registering what goes on around you. If you respond actively, you are a sensation avoider, who often feel overwhelmed by your environment, especially if it is busy and noisy with lots of people and/or activity. You may become irritable and distracted as a result. Sensation avoiders work best within established and predictable routines. They can be in tune with their environment and are often detail oriented. They need time alone on a regular basis.

Most people's profile tends to be either low or high, so it is likely that you will have significantly more marks in one column than the other. The passive and active responses are grouped together, but often, although not always, co-occur. If you have ticked more than 12 'yes' boxes in both tables, you possibly have a mixed or fluctuating profile. If you have ticked only five or less for 'yes' boxes in one or each table, you may have a typical threshold profile. This means you neither over- nor under-respond to sensory input.

Remember that you have seven senses, so it is possible that you have a low threshold for one sense (for example touch) but a high threshold for another (such as movement). I will elaborate on this component of a sensory profile when discussing the Sensory Systems Checklist in Chapter 3.

The four main sensory profiles

Now that you have determined whether you have a high or a low threshold, profile descriptions for the active or passive components will be added to help you fine-tune your profile tendencies. Remember, it is unlikely that you will be a prefect match in all components. The brain is unique and differs from individual to individual. My aim here is simply to give you a general description for each type of profile.

HIGH THRESHOLD
In this group you can be a low registrator or a sensation seeker.

Low registrators

They have high thresholds, with passive responses. Typical behavioural traits include that they:

- Take longer to respond to sensory information
- Miss environmental cues
- Appear uninterested
- Appear withdrawn
- Are conscientious
- Can focus in distracting environments
- Tend to be more flexible and comfortable in diverse environments.

Their personal needs typically include intensified stimuli and more information, and they want everything louder, brighter, tighter and faster.

Positive traits/labels	Negative traits/labels
• Good focus and attention	• 'Thick skinned'
• Conscientious	• Uninterested
• Flexible	• Ignoring others
• Easy going	• Oblivious to others
• Good endurance	• Miss detail and important information
• High levels of stamina	• Over-absorbed in their own worlds
• Day dreamers	

Best-fit jobs for low registrators include:

- Call-centre agents
- Stock traders (especially when working on a trading floor)
- Flea-market sellers
- Preschool teachers
- Open-plan office workers
- Estate agents
- Cabin crew.

Sensation seekers

They have high thresholds with active responses. Typical behavioural traits include that they:

- Seek out and create additional environmental stimuli
- Are active and 'on the go'
- Are continuously engaging
- Experience sensations as pleasurable

- Are easily bored
- Are fidgety, easily distracted, show poor concentration
- Are excitable and energetic.

Their personal needs typically include activity, novelty, variety and change. They want more information and everything needs to be louder, brighter, tighter and faster.

Positive traits/labels	Negative traits/labels
• Lively, energetic	• Cannot pin them down
• High activity levels	• Easily bored
• High levels of endurance	• Fidgety, distractible
• Daring and risk takers	• Poor concentration
• Enjoys change	• Miss detail
• Fun	• Impulsive
• Adaptable	• May become angry and aggressive quickly
• Express emotions easily	• Can have addictive traits
• Open to new experiences, curious	

Best fit-jobs for sensation seekers include:
- Tour guides
- Formula-one racers
- Pre-school teachers
- Entrepreneurs
- Open-plan office workers
- Actors, dancers
- Journalist
- CEO of a company with many travelling assignments
- Sales and marketing
- Police and rescue workers.

LOW THRESHOLDS
In this group you may be sensory sensitive or a sensation avoider.

Sensory sensitive
They have low thresholds with passive responses. Typical behavioural traits of individuals in this group include that they:
- Are easily affected by environmental stimuli
- Are irritable and easily distracted

- Show discomfort with sensory input
- Show a high level of awareness and are in tune with their environment
- Can be detail orientated.

Their personal needs include a reduction in the intensity or quantity of stimuli and they need less information, with everything softer, slower, gentler.

Positive traits/labels	Negative traits/labels
• In tune with the environment	• Irritable
• Good observers	• Anxious
• In tune with other's needs and moods	• Fidgety, distractible
• Accurate and analytic	• Perfectionist
• Intuitive	• Shy and withdrawn
• Gentle and calming	• Picky
• Conscientious	• Finicky
• Detail oriented	• Critical as they see faults quickly
• Artistically inclined	
• Deep thinkers	

Best fit-jobs for this group include:
- Computer programmers
- High school teachers
- Artists
- Therapists, counsellors, psychologists
- Strategists
- Human resource staff
- Systems analysts
- Researchers
- Medical doctors.

Sensation avoiders

They have low thresholds with active responses. Typical behavioural traits of individuals in this group include that they:
- Are overwhelmed or bothered by stimuli
- Avoid environmental stimuli/engage to reduce stimuli
- Resist change
- Rely on rigid rituals to increase predictability
- Are good at establishing structure and routine.

Their personal needs include:
- Quiet surroundings and clear expectations
- Quiet time and personal space
- Less information, softer, slower, gentler
- Structure and predictability, sameness and routine.

Positive traits/labels	Negative traits/labels
• Excellent planners	• Controlling
• Logical and sequential	• Rigid
• Predictable	• Nit picking
• Assertive	• Anxious
• Grounded	• Negative
• Stable	• Argumentative
• Secure and established	• Can't tolerate change
• Solid	• Pushy
	• Aggressive

Best-fit jobs for this group include:
- Lawyers
- Advocates
- Accountants
- Writers
- Farmers
- Systems analysts and developers
- Librarians.

Looking at elaborate job descriptions is important to establish whether you are on track with your primitive sensory needs. There are obviously a much wider range of jobs that could fit in each quadrant based on the type and structure of the job. The aim of the best-fit job listing is to identify the type of job that may work, but the environment also needs to be considered. It is always the best solution to combine your job expectations and environment to best match your sensory profile. Also remember, the trick is to match your sensory needs within your current job description. Can you change your job environment or tasks to suit your sensory needs? We will revisit these aspects in Chapter 8.

Do not dwell on the negative labels of your profile. I had to bring them in, because they have been fairly consistent and prominent in my case studies. Also, knowing our weaknesses is an opportunity for growth and development. Focus on the positive traits of your profile; it will be an excellent indication of what you do best, where you are most happy and where to use your resources optimally. The bottom line is, if you act on your sensory needs according to your profile, chances are that you will live your passions and find you dreams.

To every child I have ever worked with, it was through you that I learnt the true value of sensory integration and seeing you blossom into a new person was the biggest gift.

To every adult client, thank you for sharing your valuable stories with me and letting me into your life.

CHAPTER 3

The sensory systems

We are continuously processing information from the environment through our seven senses. The senses provide the gateway through which the brain can act on the world around us. As mentioned before, when referring to the senses most people think of the five visible senses of sight, hearing, smell, taste and touch. Our two hidden senses of movement, the vestibular sense and the proprioceptive sense are much less familiar but every bit as important.

Now that you have determined your general sensory profile, it is important to look more closely at your individual sensory systems. Each of your seven senses functions in a unique way and you have a specific threshold for each. It is important to establish to which sensory inputs you are sensitive (because you'll probably want to avoid these whenever you can) or which inputs you are seeking (because these you will probably want to add to your daily life). Looking at each of the senses separately will be particularly helpful for those who identified a mixed sensory profile, or normal thresholds (meaning neither or low nor high).

I developed the Sensory Systems Checklist which you can use to paint a more detailed picture of your sensory profile. With this checklist you can identify your tendencies within all sensory systems. This eliminates discrepancies and is valuable in identifying the best methods for self-regulation. The brain potentially uses the high threshold systems which can tolerate more to override the low threshold systems that tend to become overloaded quickly. Your lowest threshold systems are likely to be your sensory stressors, put you into sensory overload and turn your world upside down. On the other hand, the high threshold systems point to the brain's primitive need for increased sensory input and often then self-regulate the other sensory systems. Remember you can be a sensation seeker for movement, for example, but at the same time be sensory sensitive for noise. Study the sample checklist before completing your own checklist.

THE SENSORY SYSTEMS CHECKLIST

Name: *Mr Nobody*
Date: *2007-03-05*

Completing this checklist will enable you to explore and identify your threshold pattern for each sensory system and add insight into your general quadrant profile.

How do your different senses work?
1. **Smell/Taste processing:** Measure responses to odours/aromas and tastes.
2. **Visual processing:** Measure responses to what is seen.
3. **Touch processing:** Measure responses to stimuli that touch the skin.
4. **Auditory processing:** Measure responses to what is heard.
5. **Movement processing:** Measure responses to vestibular (sense of balance in the inner ear) and proprioceptive (body sense – muscles and joints) stimuli.
6. **Activity level:** Measure individual's disposition toward involvement in daily activities.

Method
Work through the checklists for the following six systems and tick what is generally applicable to your personal processing style. Some would not be applicable; do not mark them. Circle either +1 or -1 next to each box you have ticked. Count the number of behaviours where you circled either +1 or -1 for each system, write that down, then calculate your final score and add it into the shaded score block. Once you have completed the check lists for all the senses, transfer all scores from the shaded boxes to your summary score sheet.

Scores with a +, indicate high thresholds; the higher the number, the higher the threshold. Scores with a -, indicate low thresholds; the higher the number, the lower the threshold. Scores around 0 indicate typical or normal threshold responses. High threshold systems mean you can tolerate sensory input from these systems more easily; low threshold systems indicate your 'fragile' systems, where you can tolerate less sensory input, which you would be inclined to remove or avoid.

Example:

1. Smell/Taste processing

Sensation seeking

☑ Add spice to food	(+1)
☐ Enjoy being close to people who wear perfume	+1
☐ Will go to smell objects, flowers	+1
☑ Like to try new foods that have never been tasted before	(+1)
☑ Enjoy the smell of burning incense, candles, fragrant oils, etc.	(+1)

Low registration

☑ Don't smell things others smell	(+1)
☑ Many foods taste bland	(+1)
☑ Not aware of smells or odours in my environment	(+1)
☑ Not able to distinguish between smells easily	(+1)
☑ Not able to distinguish between tastes easily	(+1)

Total for + high	+8

TOTAL SCORE: calculate the sum of high and low scores	+8

Total for − low	0

Sensory sensitive

☐ Prefer familiar, bland foods, often order the same food at restaurants	-1
☐ Dislike spicy foods, strong tasting mints, sour gums, etc.	-1
☐ Usually smell odours long before other people notice them	-1
☐ Bothered by and overly sensitive to smells, perfumes, air fresheners, etc.	-1
☐ Identify smells and tastes much quicker than others	-1

Sensation avoiding

☐ Will move away from smell sections; candles/bath products, etc. in a shop	-1
☐ Only eat familiar food	-1
☐ Dislike wearing perfume	-1
☐ Avoid spicy food and/or unknown food types	-1
☐ Get nauseated by certain smells and/or tastes	-1

2. Visual processing

Sensation seeking

☑ Like and prefer places with lots of people and activities (+1)

☑ Prefer busy, moving computer screen savers (+1)

☑ Like places that have bright lights and are colourful (+1)

☑ Like to wear colourful clothing (+1)

☑ Enjoy bright light; would always open windows/blinds/curtains (+1)

Low registration

☐ Do not notice people coming into a room +1

☑ Not tuned into small details (+1)

☐ Cannot find objects in/on cluttered drawers/desks or room +1

☐ Miss street signs, buildings or room signs when trying to go somewhere new, get lost easily +1

☐ Tendency to stare at objects and/or people without being aware of it +1

Total for + high	+6

TOTAL SCORE: calculate the sum of high and low scores	+4

Total for – low	-2

Sensory sensitive

☐ Get distracted by too much visual input -1

☐ Bothered by bright and/or fluorescent lights -1

☐ Get distracted in places with many people, activities -1

☑ Bothered by fast moving visual images on TV or in movies (-1)

☑ Bothered by fast moving images when driving in a car (-1)

Sensation avoiding

☐ Prefer gentle, soft and uniform colours -1

☐ Prefer shades/blinds down or curtains closed -1

☐ Limit distractions while working – close the door, remove clutter -1

☐ Choose to shop in smaller stores where fewer visual stimuli are found, as large stores are overwhelming -1

☐ Prefer to be/enjoy being in the dark -1

3. Touch processing

Sensation seeking

☑ Enjoy and seek out hugs, kisses, touch from others	(+1)
☑ Will touch people when talking to them, touch often used as a non-verbal cue	(+1)
☑ Often touch and fiddle with objects	(+1)
☐ Like going barefoot	+1
☑ Like the feel of hair being cut	(+1)

Low registration

☑ Do not notice when hands/face are dirty	(+1)
☑ Get scrapes and bruises without remembering how	(+1)
☐ Don't seem to notice when others touch arm or back	+1
☑ Comfortable with large groups of people	(+1)
☑ Do not mind getting messy, dirty	(+1)

Total for + high	+8

TOTAL SCORE: calculate the sum of high and low scores	+8

Total for – low	0

Sensory sensitive

☐ Dislike being kissed, touched, stroked	-1
☐ Dislike specific food textures such as trifle, yoghurt with pieces, skins of vegetables/fruit, etc.	-1
☐ Bothered by feeling in mouth in the morning after waking up	-1
☐ Prefer certain textures of clothing while feeling uncomfortable with others, bothered by clothing labels, seams, etc.	-1
☐ Find cutting and/or washing of hair especially at hairdresser uncomfortable	-1

Sensation avoiding

☐ Dislike wearing jewellery, tight clothing, using electric toothbrush	-1
☐ Avoid open windows, wind blowing on body/face	-1
☐ Avoid or wear gloves during activities like gardening, cooking, etc. where hands will get dirty and sticky	-1
☐ Have a big personal space and will move away from others when they get too close	-1
☐ Avoid standing in lines or entering full elevators because of other people being too close	-1

4. Auditory processing

Sensation seeking

☐ Enjoy and seek out noisy environments	+1
☐ Like to attend events with lots of music	+1
☐ Open windows or doors to let sounds in	+1
☐ Turn up radio, TV, music	+1
☐ Hum, whistle, sing or make noises	+1

Low registration

☐ Can work with background noise and seek opportunities to add noise to work environment	+1
☐ Have trouble following what other people are saying when they talk fast or about unfamiliar topics	+1
☐ Have to ask people to repeat things	+1
☐ Don't notice when your name is called	+1
☐ Often described as being 'in a world of your own'	+1

Total for + high	0

TOTAL SCORE: calculate the sum of high and low scores	-4

Total for – low	-4

Sensory sensitive

☐ Easily bothered by noise	-1
☐ Easily startled by unexpected noise	-1
☐ Dislike loud environments – crowds, rock concerts, loud parties, etc.	-1
☑ Find it difficult to work with background noise	(-1)
☑ Distracted when there is a lot of noise around	(-1)

Sensation avoiding

☐ Withdraw from loud and fluctuating noise	-1
☑ Will leave room when others are watching TV or ask for it to be turned down	(-1)
☐ Use strategies to drown out noise – close door, cover ears, use earplugs, etc.	-1
☑ Will turn down radio/music especially when having to do something else	(-1)
☐ Prefer quiet, subdued environments	-1

5. Movement processing

Sensation seeking

☑ Enjoy how it feels to move about, dancing, running, etc.	(+1)
☑ Choose to engage in physical activities	(+1)
☑ Have difficulty to sit still, always have to be busy	(+1)
☐ Enjoy and participate in fast and high-impact sport activities	+1
☐ Love amusement parks, roller-coaster rides, etc.	+1

Low registration

☐ Tendency to trip or bump into things or objects	+1
☐ Unsure of footing when walking on stairs; fall, lose balance, need to hold on to rail	+1
☐ Grasp and handle objects harder than normal	+1
☐ Tendency to drop and/or break objects easily	+1
☐ Being in a head upside down position pose no threat rather enjoyment	+1

Total for + high	+3

TOTAL SCORE: calculate the sum of high and low scores	-2

Total for − low	-5

Sensory sensitive

☑ Afraid of heights	(-1)
☑ Dislike the movement of riding in a car and/or get motion sickness	(-1)
☐ Get dizzy easily	-1
☐ Sometimes get disorientated when getting up quickly	-1
☐ Prefer stationary activities; sitting, watching TV, reading quietly, etc.	-1

Sensation avoiding

☐ Avoid escalators and/or lifts because of dislike of movement	-1
☑ Dislike/avoid amusement parks	(-1)
☐ Prefer sport activities where minimum head movement occurs, such as biking, running, fishing, etc.	-1
☑ Avoid/would not try adrenaline driven sport like skydiving, bungee jumping, etc.	(-1)
☑ Diving off the high board at swimming scares you	(-1)

6. Activity level

Sensation seeking

☑ Can work on more than one task at any given time	(+1)
☑ Do things on the spur of the moment	(+1)
☑ Enjoy novel and new activities	(+1)
☑ Busy, 'on the go"	(+1)
☐ Concentration often poor, attention fluctuates, distractible	+1

Low registration

☐ Take longer than others to wake up in the morning	+1
☐ Seem slower than others when trying to follow an activity or task	+1
☐ Don't grasp jokes as quickly as others	+1
☑ Can over focus on a specific task, ignoring other stimuli for long periods	(+1)
☐ Often described as a dreamer	+1

Total for + high	+5
TOTAL SCORE: calculate the sum of high and low scores	+5
Total for − low	0

Sensory sensitive

☐ Difficulty in concentrating during meetings or seminars, notice other stimuli quickly and easily	-1
☐ Driving while talking on cellphone often difficult	-1
☐ Difficulty to multi-task	-1
☐ Prefer small and/or familiar restaurants, shops, malls	-1
☐ Prefer quiet, sedentary activities such as watching TV, reading, working on the computer	-1

Sensation avoiding

☐ Need to be forewarned of unexpected events	-1
☐ Prefer firm and rigid routines	-1
☐ Avoid crowds	-1
☐ Enjoy being alone and seek out opportunities to take time out	-1
☐ Prefer single sport activities such as rowing, climbing, biking, fishing, running	-1

Transfer all TOTAL SCORES onto the summary score sheet.

Summary score sheet for sensory systems checklist

Score		System
+10		
+9		
+8	High thresholds	Touch, smell and taste
+7		
+6		
+5		Activity level
+4		Visual
+3		
+2		
+1		
0		
-1		
-2		Movement
-3		
-4	Low thresholds	Auditory
-5		
-6		
-7		
-8		
-9		
-10		

Profile interpretation

Mr Nobody's profile indicates that his auditory system has the lowest threshold, with the strongest possibility of sensory overload. Noisy environments and situations will be likely to create discomfort, disorganization and irritability. Too much auditory input should be avoided and when avoidance is impossible, anticipation and self-regulation are required.

The next low system is movement, with slight sensitivity for input from this system. Higher thresholds are indicated for visual input and activity which means that Mr Nobody possibly has a high activity level, is always busy and on the go while enjoying or seeking out visual stimulation, whether it be reading, TV, lights or similar stimulation.

The thresholds for the touch, smell and taste systems are high at +8, meaning that self-regulation occurs best through these systems. A massage, for instance, taps into the tactile system and would potentially be a great stress relief for Mr Nobody. Getting deep, hard hugs from others would have a similar effect. Good, spicy food and strong, pleasant smells will also work well for self-regulation – a form of stress management on a primitive level.

Self-profiling

Complete your own sensory systems checklist. Work through the checklists for the six systems and tick what is generally applicable to your personal processing style. Some would not be applicable; do not mark them. Circle either +1 or -1 next to each box you have ticked. Count the number of behaviours where you circled either +1 or -1 for each system, write that down, then calculate your final score and add it into the shaded score block. Once you have completed the check lists for all the senses, transfer all scores from the shaded boxes to your summary score sheet (see page 63).

1. Smell/Taste processing

Sensation seeking

☐ Add spice to food	+1
☐ Enjoy being close to people who wear perfume	+1
☐ Will go to smell objects, flowers	+1
☐ Like to try new foods that have never been tasted before	+1
☐ Enjoy the smell of burning incense, candles, fragrant oils, etc.	+1

Low registration

☐ Don't smell things others smell	+1
☐ Many foods taste bland	+1
☐ Not aware of smells or odours in my environment	+1
☐ Not able to distinguish between smells easily	+1
☐ Not able to distinguish between tastes easily	+1

Total for + high

TOTAL SCORE: calculate the sum of high and low scores

Total for − low

Sensory sensitive

☐ Prefer familiar, bland foods, often order the same food at restaurants	-1
☐ Dislike spicy foods, strong tasting mints, sour gums, etc.	-1
☐ Usually smell odours long before other people notice them	-1
☐ Bothered by and overly sensitive to smells, perfumes, air fresheners, etc.	-1
☐ Identify smells and tastes much quicker than others	-1

Sensation avoiding

☐ Will move away from smell sections; candles/bath products, etc. in a shop	-1
☐ Only eat familiar food	-1
☐ Dislike wearing perfume	-1
☐ Avoid spicy foods and/or unknown food types	-1
☐ Get nauseated by certain smells and/or tastes	-1

2. Visual processing

Sensation seeking

☐ Like and prefer places with lots of people and activities	+1
☐ Prefer busy, moving computer screen savers	+1
☐ Like places that have bright lights and are colourful	+1
☐ Like to wear colourful clothing	+1
☐ Enjoy bright light; would always open windows/blinds/curtains	+1

Low registration

☐ Do not notice people coming into a room	+1
☐ Not tuned into small details	+1
☐ Cannot find objects in/on cluttered drawers/desks or room	+1
☐ Miss street signs, buildings or room signs when trying to go somewhere new, get lost easily	+1
☐ Tendency to stare at objects and/or people without being aware of it	+1

Total for + high

TOTAL SCORE: calculate the sum of high and low scores

Total for – low

Sensory sensitive

☐ Get distracted by too much visual input	-1
☐ Bothered by bright and/or fluorescent lights	-1
☐ Get distracted in places with many people, activities	-1
☐ Bothered by fast moving visual images on TV or in movies	-1
☐ Bothered by fast moving images when driving in a car	-1

Sensation avoiding

☐ Prefer gentle, soft and uniform colours	-1
☐ Prefer shades/blinds down or curtains closed	-1
☐ Limit distractions while working – close the door, remove clutter	-1
☐ Choose to shop in smaller stores where fewer visual stimuli are found, as large stores are overwhelming	-1
☐ Prefer to be/enjoy being in the dark	-1

3. Touch processing

Sensation seeking

☐ Enjoy and seek out hugs, kisses, touch from others	+1
☐ Will touch people when talking to them, touch often used as a non-verbal cue	+1
☐ Often touch and fiddle with objects	+1
☐ Like going barefoot	+1
☐ Like the feel of hair being cut	+1

Low registration

☐ Do not notice when hands/face are dirty	+1
☐ Get scrapes and bruises without remembering how	+1
☐ Don't seem to notice when others touch arm or back	+1
☐ Comfortable with large groups of people	+1
☐ Do not mind getting messy, dirty	+1

Total for + high

TOTAL SCORE: calculate the sum of high and low scores

Total for − low

Sensory sensitive

☐ Dislike being kissed, touched, stroked	-1
☐ Dislike specific food textures such as trifle, yoghurt with pieces, skins of vegetables/fruit, etc.	-1
☐ Bothered by feeling in mouth in the morning after waking up	-1
☐ Prefer certain textures of clothing while feeling uncomfortable with others, bothered by clothing labels, seams, etc.	-1
☐ Find cutting and/or washing of hair especially at hairdresser uncomfortable	-1

Sensation avoiding

☐ Dislike wearing jewellery, tight clothing, using electric toothbrush	-1
☐ Avoid open windows, wind blowing on body/face	-1
☐ Avoid or wear gloves during activities like gardening, cooking, etc. where hands will get dirty and sticky	-1
☐ Have a big personal space and will move away from others when they get too close	-1
☐ Avoid standing in lines or entering full elevators because of other people being too close	-1

4. Auditory processing

Sensation seeking

☐ Enjoy and seek out noisy environments	+1
☐ Like to attend events with lots of music	+1
☐ Open windows or doors to let sounds in	+1
☐ Turn up radio, TV, music	+1
☐ Hum, whistle, sing or make noises	+1

Low registration

☐ Can work with background noise and seek opportunities to add noise to work environment	+1
☐ Have trouble following what other people are saying when they talk fast or about unfamiliar topics	+1
☐ Have to ask people to repeat things	+1
☐ Don't notice when your name is called	+1
☐ Often described as being 'in a world of your own'	+1

Total for + high

TOTAL SCORE: calculate the sum of high and low scores

Total for − low

Sensory sensitive

☐ Easily bothered by noise	-1
☐ Easily startled by unexpected noise	-1
☐ Dislike loud environments – crowds, rock concerts, loud parties, etc.	-1
☐ Find it difficult to work with background noise	-1
☐ Distracted when there is a lot of noise around	-1

Sensation avoiding

☐ Withdraw from loud and fluctuating noise	-1
☐ Will leave room when others are watching TV or ask for it to be turned down	-1
☐ Use strategies to drown out noise – close door, cover ears, use earplugs, etc.	-1
☐ Will turn down radio/music especially when having to do something else	-1
☐ Prefer quiet, subdued environments	-1

5. Movement processing

Sensation seeking

☐ Enjoy how it feels to move about, dancing, running, etc.	+1
☐ Choose to engage in physical activities	+1
☐ Have difficulty to sit still, always have to be busy	+1
☐ Enjoy and participate in fast and high-impact sport activities	+1
☐ Love amusement parks, roller-coaster rides, etc.	+1

Low registration

☐ Tendency to trip or bump into things or objects	+1
☐ Unsure of footing when walking on stairs; fall, lose balance, need to hold on to rail	+1
☐ Grasp and handle objects harder than normal	+1
☐ Tendency to drop and/or break objects easily	+1
☐ Being in a head upside down position pose no threat rather enjoyment	+1

Total for + high

TOTAL SCORE: calculate the sum of high and low scores

Total for − low

Sensory sensitive

☐ Afraid of heights	-1
☐ Dislike the movement of riding in a car and/or get motion sickness	-1
☐ Get dizzy easily	-1
☐ Sometimes get disorientated when getting up quickly	-1
☐ Prefer stationary activities; sitting, watching TV, reading quietly, etc.	-1

Sensation avoiding

☐ Avoid escalators and/or lifts because of dislike of movement	-1
☐ Dislike/avoid amusement parks	-1
☐ Prefer sport activities where minimum head movement occurs, such as biking, running, fishing, etc.	-1
☐ Avoid/would not try adrenaline driven sport like skydiving, bungee jumping, etc.	-1
☐ Diving off the high board at swimming scares you	-1

6. Activity level

Sensation seeking

☐ Can work on more than one task at any given time	+1
☐ Do things on the spur of the moment	+1
☐ Enjoy novel and new activities	+1
☐ Busy, 'on the go"	+1
☐ Concentration often poor, attention fluctuates, distractible	+1

Low registration

☐ Take longer than others to wake up in the morning	+1
☐ Seem slower than others when trying to follow an activity or task	+1
☐ Don't grasp jokes as quickly as others	+1
☐ Can over focus on a specific task, ignoring other stimuli for long periods	+1
☐ Often described as a dreamer	+1

Total for + high

TOTAL SCORE: calculate the sum of high and low scores

Total for – low

Sensory sensitive

☐ Difficulty to concentrate during meetings or seminars, notice other stimuli quickly and easily	-1
☐ Driving while talking on cellphone often difficult	-1
☐ Difficulty to multi-task	-1
☐ Prefer small and/or familiar restaurants, shops, malls	-1
☐ Prefer quiet, sedentary activities such as watching TV, reading, working on the computer	-1

Sensation avoiding

☐ Need to be forewarned of unexpected events	-1
☐ Prefer firm and rigid routines	-1
☐ Avoid crowds	-1
☐ Enjoy being alone and seek out opportunities to take time out	-1
☐ Prefer single sport activities such as rowing, climbing, biking, fishing, running	-1

Transfer all TOTAL SCORES onto the summary score sheet.

Summary score sheet for sensory systems checklist

Score		System
+10		
+9		
+8		
+7		
+6	High thresholds	
+5		
+4		
+3		
+2		
+1		
0		
-1		
-2		
-3		
-4	Low thresholds	
-5		
-6		
-7		
-8		
-9		
-10		

Your system with the highest negative score is your sensory stressors, causing irritation, discomfort and should be managed well. Your system with the highest positive score is your sensory need and will potentially be best for use to self-regulate. The higher the score (+) the more you want the input, the lower the score (-), the more sensitive/defensive you are. If your score for a particular system is -1, 0 or +1 you are neither searching nor avoiding with regard to inputs and you have a normal threshold. Where there is a normal threshold for sensory input the system is balanced and accessible (overload is unlikely).

Senses on defence	Senses on demand
• LOW threshold	• HIGH threshold
• Minus scores (-2 to -10)	• Plus scores (+2 to +10)
• Sensory overload	• Sensory seeking
• Primitive need for less	• Primitive need for more
• Performance impact: more stress responses, loss of focus and attention, overload more pertinent	• Performance impact: more boredom, loss of focus and attention
• Avoiding, anticipation, planning and preparation important	• Structuring and choices of activities important

Now let's explore the sensory systems in more detail. By identifying their role in our daily interaction with the world around us, we will learn new and interesting facts, hidden and overlooked before. I will use various case studies anonymously to explain the impact of the senses on daily life issues.

The five visible senses

You know that the five visible sense are sight, hearing, smell, taste and touch. Let's look at them in more detail.

THE SMELL AND TASTE SYSTEMS

The functioning of these two systems is so closely connected that they are grouped together. You cannot have taste without smell, although, obviously, you can have smell without taste.

Living with smell and taste

Our environment is filled with smells, aromas, flavours and odours and depending on where you are or where you work, it is very difficult to avoid sensory input from this system. It is important to remind you that smell is the brain's preferential sense whose input is transferred immediately via a direct 'hotline' from the olfactory bulb (the smell receptor) to the limbic system (the emotional brain), which also stores memories. Because of this 'hotline' we experience strong emotions and specific memories as a result of smell. Environmental allergies are also identified via the sense of smell. Whether it is dust, pollens, fumes or smoke, some of us respond quite strongly to chemical particles in our environment.

The limbic system furthermore contains the brain's pleasure centres which can be activated by scents. Because our olfactory system is wired directly to our pleasure centres, it is a powerful trigger that can motivate us quickly without thinking too much about it. This link to the brain is simple, direct and powerful. Since smell accesses our memory centres so directly, we often have pleasant or unpleasant memories attached to certain smells.

I also believe that every place has a particular 'smell'. I remember when arriving in the United States for the first time I got off the plane and it was the different smell that caught my attention immediately – although I have a high threshold for smells. Every person also has a unique body odour. It is believed that babies can identify their mothers through their sense of smell rather than their sense of sight, since the visual system is poorly developed at birth.

Taste is facilitated whenever we put something in our mouths to chew and eat. Neurophysiologically we also know that smell and taste work together for identification of the taste of food. The taste buds on our tongues merely identify sweet, salty, sour or bitter. It is because of the ability of the receptors in the nostrils that we are capable of recognizing and differentiating as many as 10 000 odours. It is believed that 75% of what we taste, referring to the flavour, is actually attributed to our sense of smell. Temperature has a distinct affect on our taste mechanisms. When the tongue and the taste buds are exposed to very cold or very hot temperatures, the ability to sense certain tastes is greatly reduced.

Why do some of us like spicy foods? Brain scientists have determined that eating spicy foods triggers the release of endorphins in the brain – powerful chemicals that block pain and create a happy feeling. I have found that people with high thresholds and sensation seeking traits typically enjoy spicy and hot foods.

Another interesting neurological fact is that the brain adapts to continuous sensory input. This applies to the sense of taste, but is also true for all the other senses. The brain basically habituates (or gets used to) input that is being maintained. Isn't it true that the fifth biscuit with chilli dip has far less of a bite than the first one? When you are eating, the brain is activated every time you take a bite of a different food. If you eat a spoonful of meat, then potato, then vegetables and then meat again, the brain is 'switched on' or stimulated with every bite. But if you eat all your meat first, then your potato, then your vegetables, your brain gets used to the taste of the particular food and after the fourth of fifth bite there is less activity in that circuitry in the brain. I find it interesting that sensation avoiders consistently eat their foods 'compartmentally' – first the meat, then the potatoes, then the vegetables. And generally they don't mix their food on their plates.

The most common complaints in the area of smell are that people avoid certain environments at all costs. Examples are the soap or candle aisles in department stores – any place where smell, scent or aroma is used in an effort to sell a product. A trickier situation is feeling uncomfortable and yes, sometimes even nauseous when entering someone's home or a particular workspace. If you find the smell of their environment particularly unpleasant, you will not be very social nor friendly. I have many clients who simply avoid visiting certain people because of the smell surrounding their environment. And the person 'responsible for the smell' feels rejected. Smell sensitive individuals also usually avoid wearing perfume, cologne, perfumed lotions or creams, and obviously don't enjoy being close to others wearing these. Bear in mind that your smell sensitive girlfriend or wife will not enjoy a strongly fragrant bunch of flowers nor a bottle of expensive perfume with an overpowering fragrance.

Smell seekers on the other end surround themselves with smells from perfume, burning incense, perfumed candles, etc. Taste seekers enjoy spicy and hot foods and experiment with new food. They turn any trip to a different country into a culinary experience and enjoy tasting new foods with excitement and zest.

The senses of smell and taste play a big role in individuals developing an aversion to certain foods. However, touch sensitivity to food textures seems to coincide with an oral-defensive pattern which in many cases actually aggravates the sensitivity to foods. I will elaborate on this when we discuss the touch system.

Case studies on smell and taste stressors

Mary*, a 28 year old woman, with a significant sensory avoiding profile and sensitivities to touch, taste, smell and auditory input, had to go to an island with her husband for a church outreach. Before leaving she gained as much knowledge as possible about their eating habits (which is a good strategy) but she actually only ate rice while on the 10-day trip. She just could not get herself to eat their particular foods which were spicy, mashed, with an eastern flair.

Andrea*, a 40 year old female with the same profile as Mary, hated going out to dinner parties to her friends' homes. She was labelled 'picky and fussy' and was hurt by the fact that people just would not invite her because it was so difficult to please her with food. For Andrea it was important to get rid of this label and in counselling I recommended that she try new foods in her own home, where it is okay to spit it out. We used the brain's ability to habituate so that she could desensitize her taste and smell systems through continued exposure. It did improve significantly. Andrea will never be an adventurous eater, but managed to eat some foods she had always avoided before.

Thandi* is a 35 year old female executive working in human resources for a large company. She was on a panel to interview and select a candidate for a senior position at their firm. Although it bothered no one else, Thandi was overwhelmed by the body odour of one particular candidate. She found it very offensive and although he had all the qualities to fill the position successfully, she just could not support the team recommending him for the position and his application was rejected. She did not share the reasons for her reluctance with her colleagues, feeling too embarrassed about it since none of them commented on the applicant's body odour.

Avoid or self-regulate through smell and taste

If your score on the Sensory Systems Checklist was between -2 and -10 it means that you are sensitive to smell and taste. Avoiding strong smells and tastes would therefore be the best way to address your sensory needs in the smell/taste system:

- Use bland food with fewer spices
- Avoid using strong perfumes, lotions, soaps
- Buy non-fragrant bath-care and skin-care products or products with a less powerful smells
- Burn scented candles that work for you – it will alleviate the other smells to an extent
- Don't work in a fish factory
- Regularly air your home/office to alleviate smells
- When cooking, switch on your extractor fan, and/or open the window
- Introduce new smells or foods slowly and gradually to cope with specific demands.

Although taste is easily manipulated, smell proves to be trickier. We determine what we put into our mouths, but the release of smell chemicals in the atmosphere and environment around us are far more difficult to avoid. I usually despair for someone with a severe smell sensitivity because I know it is one of the most difficult senses to work with, owing to the brain hotline.

If your score on the Sensory Systems Checklist was between +2 and +10, you can choose smell and taste to self-regulate. Especially if your highest threshold was smell and taste, your system would self-regulate best through smell and taste. The possibilities are endless and should form part of your sensory diet:

Smell

- Aromatherapy using pleasant smells to release stress and create a sense of well-being
- Burn fragrant candles or incense
- Use fragrant lotions, soaps, bath salts, shampoos, perfume
- Use air fresheners in your home, car or office (just consider the people sharing your space – they may be smell sensitive)
- Plant a herb garden or plants with distinct smells.

Taste

- Cook up a storm with strong smelling, delicious foods
- Use spices liberally
- Go wine tasting
- Visit food festivals and taste everything

- Go out for dinner, trying new restaurants and/or new foods
- Have a romantic dinner for two at home, cooking your favourite flavourful dishes
- Chew gum.

A word of caution: Food should be savoured and enjoyed slowly like the French do. Eating indiscriminately as a stress-management tool is never recommended as it has significant health risks. Healthy eating with a balanced diet will regulate your system, add energy and manage your stress significantly. What I am suggesting here is using particular tastes in an enjoyable, yet responsible way without overeating.

THE VISUAL SYSTEM

The eyes hold one of our key and most important senses for interpreting the world.

Living with the visual system

We see, we interpret, and we act. The visual system is the main sense (together with hearing) which we use to access new information. Think about you sitting in a class or lecture; it is through seeing and hearing that new information is being processed and you gain knowledge. Although the senses for smell, taste, touch and movement are also important, they act in a supporting role, keeping your body together to maintain equilibrium with the physical environment. But the eyes and ears are used to pick up information and learn.

The visual brain process is intricate and fascinating. For the purpose of looking at visual modulation, we are more interested in what happens with the filtering and processing of information in receptors, visual pathway and lower parts of the brain rather than the highly complicated parts of what the cortex is actually doing with the information. I would like to stress these important points:
- Every person's brain is unique
- Some brains feel overloaded by too much visual information while other brains thrive on more visual information.

Everyone's brain is unique. We do not see, process and interpret visual information in the same way others do. I have a simple, well-known example to illustrate this. Look at the image on the next page with its black blotches on a white background. Study it carefully. Can you see what it is?

Some of us will immediately see that it is a cowboy on a horse without being told it is. Some of us will see it when given the verbal, cognitive clue that it is a cowboy on a horse. Some of us will only see it when given a guide on the picture and then concentrating very hard. Others will just not see it.

This confirms the fact that our brains are different, and process information in a unique way. There is no right or wrong; there is only different. This is crucial to know for us to develop understanding for those around us.

If you have scores from +2 to +10 on the Sensory Systems Checklist it is most probable that your brain is stimulated by visual information and you potentially enjoy seeing things or experiencing things through the eyes in overload environments. The opposite is true for those with scores of -2 to -10 on the Sensory Systems Checklist. Your brain tends to become overloaded with too much visual information and you avoid clutter, bright lights, moving objects in front of the eyes, and busy environments where there are potentially many activities and people.

The eyes interpret the world through objects in our environment. However, we cannot consider the visual system without noting two further important aspects which form part of our environment and have been known through research to impact on how the eyes perform in every day living.

The effect of light and glare

From an evolutionary perspective we need sunlight; our forefathers hunted or gathered during the day and slept at night. Then Thomas Edison developed the light bulb and brought light into our homes. The world started to distinguish between natural lighting and artificial lighting. The brain has a particular structure called the pineal gland which responds particularly to sunlight. Depression is known to be more common in people living in areas with reduced light, especially sunlight or natural light. Light therapy was shown to uplift their emotional status. Research has also been done on the positive effect of natural lighting on performance as opposed to fluorescent lighting.

Glare from high gloss work surfaces, walls and floors is known to contribute to optical fatigue and result in reduced work performance. People working at computer workstations in particular are quite susceptible to various sources of glare.

The effect of colour

There is an entire industry using the concept of colour to manipulate mood, performance and social interaction, and the psychological effect of colour has been well documented. I know for a fact that some of my individual clients with low visual thresholds are sensitive to yellow and prefer purple. I certainly believe in considering the effect of colour, lighting and glare for office areas as these aspects of visual input have a marked effect on attention, fatigue and performance. The problem is just finding optimal suitability for a wider group of people. There are general principles to apply with colour and lighting, but there will always be individuals who do not fit the general mould and may prefer the opposite. You may want to further investigate this interesting subject.

Case studies on visual stressors

Linda* is a 42-year old woman I've coached through disorganization and sensory overload resulting from a strongly sensory defensive profile. When I compiled her history, she shared the rituals she went through when commuting on the underground while living in New York. "I would put on my heaviest, darkest coat, with the collar turned upwards. I would spray my own perfume on a scarf and cover my neck, head and a part of my face. I would put on ear phones and listen to music, have my sunglasses on and read the newspaper. I tried to cocoon myself to get away from all the sights, sounds and smells on the train." Visual overload together with smell, auditory and tactile overload were problems for Linda. She had to use these rituals to cope with the commute which had to happen every morning. Wearing the sunglasses and reading the paper was a way to visually exclude other information in her environment. Her heavy coat and scarf were for tactile protection, her own perfume for smell protection and the music for avoiding auditory overload.

Steve* is an executive management member of a large corporation. Meetings are a nightmare as Steve is so visually sensitive that he cannot have the lights on in the boardroom. The problem is that while Steve prefers to be in semi-darkness, his colleagues need the light on to prime their brains, and to feel awake and alert and be able to communicate. (Bright light is known to alert or stimulate the brain, while dimmed light is calming for the brain.) This created quite a difficult scenario and choices of boardroom or meeting venues became a problem. Whenever fluorescent lights needed to be switched on, Steve got irritated. He was literally responding to his primitive brain going into self-protection. The installation of individually controlled down lights for each seating position in the boardroom was implemented which dealt with the issue effectively.

The great American architect, Buckminster Fuller, well known for developing the geodesic dome, often had tremendous visual overload. He wore glasses that would allow only partial visual information to reach his eyes and found it easier to think when he had his glasses on. He also wore earplugs when outside on a building site or in the city as he could not cope with the noise.

Avoid or self-regulate through the visual system

I believe the biggest advantage of this system is that we can switch it off. Although thanks to the unconscious mind and memory your brain enables you to visualize without actually seeing, what better way to reduce optical fatigue than to simply close your eyes. It is the easiest, yet most effective way to reduce visual overload. None of the other senses can actually be switched off. Think about it – smell, touch, movement and sound are constant. Taste you can manipulate because it is your choice whether you put something in your mouth or not, but apart from taste and vision, all other sensory systems are always subconsciously working in response to continuous input from the receptors.

If your score on the Sensory Systems Checklist for visual thresholds was between -2 and -10 it means that you are sensitive to visual input. The following strategies will help you avoid visual sensory overload:

- Avoid visual overload by closing your eyes and relaxing
- Reduce clutter around you; maintain a less is more approach
- Organize drawers, cupboards, working spaces for easier identification
- Use soft, gentle, calming colours such as light blues, greens, purples
- When fluorescent lighting is used, consider full-spectrum lighting which causes less irritation to the eyes
- Use symmetry or simple patterns when decorating
- Use full-spectrum lighting or natural colours in your workspace
- Use a blank screen saver
- Wear sunglasses when you are outdoors
- A cap or hat may help to exclude an excess of visual information

- Close the blinds or curtains
- Use tinted film on your windows to reduce glare.

If your score on the Sensory Systems Checklist for visual was anything between +2 and +10, you possibly self-regulate effectively through the visual system and the following would be beneficial and should be part of your sensory diet:
- Use visual calmers such as fish tanks, lava lamps and oil and water toys
- Read
- Watch movies
- Participate in art activities such as drawing classes, pottery, quilt making, etc. where lots of colour and medium are used
- Incorporate bright lights, and contrasting shapes and forms in your décor
- Switch on the light, open the window or blind
- Visit museums, carnivals, flea markets, etc.
- Install an exciting screen saver for your PC.

THE TOUCH/TACTILE SYSTEM

Touch is the first sense to develop and the primary receptors infants rely on for connecting with the world. Our touch receptors are located in the skin. As we have skin from the top of our heads right down to the soles of our feet, the touch system has the biggest receptor area of all the sensory systems. Touch receptors are also more densely packed in the mouth, face, hands and soles of the feet. The densely packed receptors in the hands are useful since we need to identify and distinguish the properties of objects largely through our hands. The density of touch receptors in the mouth may be the key to explaining why so many individuals with touch sensitivity also has oral sensitivity with particular food aversions, mostly based on texture. The sensations of pain, pressure and temperature are also relayed via touch receptors.

Living with touch

Being touched and cuddled by their mothers encourages the development of the nervous system in babies. They rely heavily on touch to bond, to find the mother's breast for feeding and for the development of motor skills. There is lots of research showing the advantage of touch and massage in advancing the development and growth of pre-term babies. Research done in orphanages in Romania found that the babies who were left in cribs and never touched suffered from stunted growth.

Living with touch has various aspects that I am certain you haven't thought about:

Physical contact and socialization

Is it the tactile sense that guides us towards physical interaction with others? How big is your personal body space? Can you tolerate people in your face or do you prefer to have them at a distance? Do you tend to touch people when you talk to them? Do you enjoy hugs and kisses? We use our tactile sense for non-verbal communication and we interact with others subconsciously through our sense of touch. Children with tactile sensitivity and tactile defensiveness have been shown to have problems relating with their peers on a social level. Among touch sensitive adults, too, there is a marked sense of being a loner, preferring and needing time on their own and avoiding crowds or situations where lots of people are present. Individuals with high touch thresholds on the other hand, tend to enjoy touch, would touch others while talking to them and enjoy situations where many people are involved. They are avid huggers and have an insignificant personal body space.

If individuals in an intimate relationship have different tactile thresholds, there is potential for conflict and feelings of rejection. I often work with clients who are tactile defensive or whose partners are tactile defensive. If your partner is tactile defensive and avoids touch and finds cuddling potentially stressful, you may often experience a feeling of rejection. The person who is tactile defensive finds touch potentially uncomfortable and the brain's fight/flight or fright responses are often triggered, making these withdrawal responses automatic and unconscious. Understanding of, and insight into, tactile thresholds are crucial within any relationship and will help you move away from labelling and feeling rejected. This can bring a new dimension to a relationship where one partner is tactile defensive.

Personal care

The tactile system determines how comfortable or irritated you feel with anything around and on you that stimulates the brain by touching the skin. The feel of clothing, jewellery, skin-care products, make-up and hair products gives specific feedback through the brain via the tactile receptors. Bear in mind that low threshold individuals take in more information; that is why basic touch information through the skin can often cause irritation and discomfort. They are over-responding to normal daily touch input. Low-threshold individuals typically
- Avoid tight clothing
- Avoid woollen, scratchy fabrics, rather preferring soft cottons
- Avoid new clothes unless washed first as items may feel scratchy
- Find polo necks and G-strings uncomfortable
- Regard pantihose as a definite no-no
- Are irritated by sock seams and/or labels and need to remove labels or wear socks inside out or seamless

- Prefer liquid soap to bars of soap
- Bath/shower twice or more a day or would strongly prefer to bath or shower more than once a day
- Do not like to be dirty and avoid handling raw meat, some vegetables and fruit
- Dislike gardening because of having to touch and work with soil
- Avoid dangling ear rings, bangles or necklaces, often just wearing a watch or a wedding ring
- Prefer a simple hairstyle, often long and away from the face to minimize tactile contact in the face area
- Hate going to the hairdresser and often have a sensitive scalp. They prefer a familiar hairdresser who can work quickly and get it done
- Dislike or avoid combing hair, filing or cutting nails
- Are uncomfortable with shaving as it creates pain and discomfort to the skin
- Dislike the feeling of lotions or creams on the body and/or face
- Avoid using make-up
- Dislike or feel irritated by the movement of the hairs on the skin by moving air such as fans, vents, air conditioners.

Often coinciding with tactile sensitivity is oral motor sensitivity in the mouth area. Sensitive individuals typically

- Prefer a manual to an electric toothbrush owing to the intense feeling of vibration in the mouth
- Find flossing teeth highly uncomfortable
- Dislike certain food textures. Often slimy, mushy textures with variations in texture seem to be culprits. Trifle with its many textures and layers seems to be very off-putting. Every single orally defensive person I've come across rate trifle the number one worst food and would not even consider eating it
- Often do not mix food on their plate when they eat.

Case studies on touch stressors

Mary*, a 28 year old woman, with a significant sensory defensive profile and sensitivities for touch, taste, smell and auditory input was mentioned before. She is disorganized, struggles to control her emotions and often feels overwhelmed by life. She finds it very hard to wake up in the morning and is extremely fussy with food. Her mother told her that she was an extremely fussy and difficult baby. Her mother always had to cook special food for her, different from that of the rest of the family. She prefers bland food and will eat meat, rice and potatoes every day. She hates eating salads and find them too crunchy and cold. She never mixes her food on her plate. She is fussy with clothing, preferring to wear soft cottons. She does not wear any jewellery and would take off her watch, wedding ring and shoes whenever she can. She wears her hair very long and always tied back, uses no make-up and no wash cloths or sponges when she baths. These are all classic signs of extreme sensitivity in the tactile system. Mary finds it difficult to self-regulate and she would often zone out when the world gets too much for her. She home schools her children and finds her own home environment calming and safe.

Wendy*, a 24-year old manager of a childcare facility, approached me after she attended a workshop on sensory intelligence for parents. While discussing touch and oral defensiveness, I referred to the possible link between anorexia nervosa and oral defensiveness. As a result Wendy shared her personal history of anorexia with me and became a client soon after. She is sensory defensive to touch, oral and auditory input in particular. She grew up in a wonderful, stable home and when she was diagnosed with anorexia as a teenager, everyone was baffled, including her. None of the emotional trauma and psychological profiles usually associated with anorexia fitted her. For the first time Wendy had a possible explanation for the origin of her anorexia: tactile and especially oral defensiveness. She admitted that she literally has to force herself to eat during times of stress as she finds the food textures in her mouth awful. Food makes her nauseous and she gags. She usually eats as fast as possible. She cannot stand going into a shopping mall or buying groceries and avoids public crowded places as much as possible. In her words: "They touch me!" She feels dirty very quickly and showers/baths twice a day and if she can, more than twice a day.

Anna* is a 44-year old woman, living at home with her husband. Her two children have left home and live on their own. She describes herself as a difficult, fussy person who tends to be introspective. She enjoys social contact with people, but wants to be in control and the people and situations should be predictable. Anna hates being hot, she has an air conditioner in her room and always has to have it set as cold as possible. She avoids being touched by others, prefers soft textures for clothing and blankets, always takes her shoes off and does not cook regularly as she hates having her hands dirty. She hates haircuts and will brush her hair quickly and as seldom as possible. She will never use an electric toothbrush. She is a perfectionist, who likes to control her world and her house is super tidy and clean. She was the administrator of an old-age home and coped well with her work as it was structured and she could work flexi-time. She found sitting in front of the TV with her husband very difficult as it was too loud and noisy for her. We introduced a sensory diet and self-regulation strategies for her; she started knitting while watching TV with her husband which improved her threshold for the auditory input.

Avoid or self-regulate through touch

If your score on the Sensory Systems Checklist for touch was between -2 and -10 it means that you are possibly tactile defensive. The following strategies will help you avoid tactile sensory overload:

- Choose your clothing carefully and avoid scratchy fabrics
- Buy seamless socks
- Cut out labels
- When seated in a group or at a restaurant, choose a corner or at the back where you can see who is in front of you and minimize possible touch from behind. Touch from behind is unexpected and particularly stressful as it immediately triggers the automatic fight/fright/flight response
- Avoid g-strings, polo necks, pantihose or other clothing restricting and snug fitting clothing – it will irritate you
- If you feel irritated, think what the cause might be and remove it if possible (please just don't strip in public)
- Use the stairs if your only other option is a crowded lift – by doing this you will self-regulate through the movement system and it will keep you fit and healthy
- If you want to try out food that might be a potential problem, try cold rather than warm temperature as cold numbs the tactile receptors in the mouth and it is usually better tolerated. Or suck on an ice cube before eating something new
- Touch food before eating it. This helps with familiarising and desensitizing
- Wear gloves when gardening, washing dishes or handling dirty objects (this does not count for your kids)
- Avoid busy malls on a Saturday morning. Go on Tuesday morning at 10 or late at night, better even, do Internet shopping
- Avoid dangling jewellery and wispy hairstyles that tickle the face
- Avoid air from fans or air conditioning vents that blow directly on you
- It is okay and very useful to tell people close to you if you find the sensation of their beard, soft kiss, light touch, etc. irritating. You will be identifying the stressor, not insult the person
- Carrying a back pack will give you some breathing space when standing in a line and waiting
- Deep hugs are easier to tolerate than light touch.

If your score on the Sensory Systems Checklist for tactile input was between +2 and +10, you possibly self-regulate effectively through the tactile system and the following activities may be beneficial and should be part of your sensory diet:

- Incorporate a regular massage into your schedule
- Participate in sport involving touch, for example, swimming, diving, contact sport
- Hug your loved ones daily. And if they're tactile defensive, ask first, hug deep and hard and let go quickly!
- Use textures liberally in your home, office, car – wobbly, beady car seats may feel great for a tactile sensation seeker
- Textured carpets, towels, clothing or blankets can be particularly enjoyable
- Indulge in gardening or cooking; they are multi-sensory experiences with especially tactile input
- Walk barefoot to enhance sensation through the feet (remember that tactile defensive people also sometimes prefer going barefoot as they dislike the feeling of socks or shoes)
- Use a face or body scrub with a coarse texture
- Use a loofah or brush to enhance your shower/bath experience.

THE AUDITORY SYSTEM

The auditory sense is a primary sense we use on a daily basis to process information that we hear from the environment. It is vital for communication, interaction and performance.

Living with sound

Our ears are switched on 24/7 meaning that our sound receptors are constantly ready and alert to absorb sound waves from the environment. Owing to modern technology most of us live in noise-polluted environments. We cannot escape the sound-loaded hustle and bustle of city living. To add to these sound inputs, there has been an extensive move to open-plan office environments over the past few decades. Although it has many benefits, the impact on the performance of auditory sensitive people in the workplace has not been sufficiently considered. Workspaces are filled with electronic noise from phones, faxes, computers, printers, air conditioners, etc.

Many people are parents. Small children are loud, busy and noisy. When they get older we have to tolerate their choice, intensity and volume of music. Noise sensitivity is something very real and many of my clients complain of auditory overload at home, in the office and in other environments. We can never turn off sound. You may be asleep at night, then be woken up by something. You know you've heard something but owing to the 'sleep state' of your brain you can't identify it. However, your auditory system was activated and triggered via the primitive brain to wake you up.

"I live in a noise-polluted area" was the comment made by a client who decided to move to a rural town to try to escape all the noise from city living.

I am sure that our environment determines the amount of auditory overload we experience. Auditory overload ratings would potentially be more severe in a city area than a rural area. Within the boundaries of any living area, there would potentially be a number of people who are sensitive to noise and experience overload as a result. However, there's an equally large number of people who enjoy the noisy and busy lifestyle. Although environment plays a major role, your genetic neurological thresholds are the most important and powerful contributor to sensitivity.

I have identified various noise stressors in my practice as reported by my clients. These stressors vary greatly from person to person. Each individual's auditory sensitivity is unique, specific and different based on their genetic predisposition and exposure.

Common auditory stressors and irritations include:

- The popcorn brigade at the movies (those scratching like hens in their huge popcorn containers) is a huge noise irritation for the noise sensitives. However, people with high noise thresholds are oblivious to them, probably crunching along loudly
- The sound of someone eating, usually in close proximity; imagine dinner time at the table
- The sound of phones, faxes, printers, air conditioners, computers in the workplace
- The pitch, rhythm and frequency of people's voices
- The sound of data projectors and/or air conditioners at conferences, workshops, lecturers and/or seminars
- Household noises like vacuum cleaners, hair dryers, etc. It seems that noise with a higher pitch and frequency tend to be more difficult to manage
- Dogs barking
- Taps dripping
- Ticking sounds of clocks
- Music, TV
- Cars, traffic, sirens
- Aeroplanes
- Machinery with low vibrations.

Case studies on auditory stressors

Didi*, a 36 year old advocate contacted me a while back after an article I wrote on sensory defensiveness was published in a local magazine. "I read your article and know now why my husband and I got divorced!" she said over the phone. This marked the beginning of my journey with this highly intelligent woman with severe sensory sensitivity to auditory, tactile, visual, smell and taste input. She experienced a lack of energy and always felt overwhelmed and stressed. Her medical history included anxiety, depression, chronic fatigue, sleep disturbances and skin disorder. While giving me her background history, Didi told me the following: "I am excruciatingly sensitive to noise. When the lawn is being mowed, I get in my car and drive away until it is over. A barking dog two blocks away drives me mad. I don't allow a vacuum cleaner in my house. I can hear an electronic alarm clock beeping 150 metres away through glass." She longed for peace and quiet, but being married to a musician in a rock band made this virtually impossible. Didi and her husband got divorced after four years of marriage, as they were just not compatible on a sensory level. The first thing she did after he moved out was to get rid of their TV.

Didi also struggles to cope with her very cute, lively, and yes noisy, little three-year-old daughter. "My noise sensitivity creates great tension between my little girl and myself. I get jumpy and cranky when she does the normal three-year-old things such as shouting, dropping things, banging doors, etc. Sometimes I shout at her to stop. I experience severe panic and stress during sudden noise." Didi avoids going out, taking her daughter for a walk, etc. as the change of scenery and environment adds to her visual overload. "I really battle with being overloaded. I feel 'flooded'. It plays havoc in my life. It damages my relationships. I am a loner because social settings exhaust me. My daughter suffers because I nag or shout at her not to make a noise." Her work schedule during court cases also impacted on her time and stress levels extensively.

It was vital for Didi to restructure her life, work and activities. She moved out of chambers into a home office with great success; thereby she avoided traffic and commuting and could contain her workspace effortlessly. She relies heavily on three au pairs working shifts to help take care her daughter. The brushing programme (see Chapter 7) together with other strategies and interventions were introduced successfully to Didi to improve her coping mechanisms and desensitize her to some sensory input.

Avoid or self-regulate through the auditory system

There are huge amounts of research confirming the positive and healing effects of music. Whether you have low or high thresholds for the auditory system, music is something that can be used by both groups owing to the modulatory effect of certain types of music on the brain. Music should be carefully selected by those with low thresholds and noise sensitivity. Baroque music, especially Mozart, and Gregorian chants seem to be particularly calming and organizing for the brain. Many sound-healing concepts today are based on the early work of Dr Alfred Tomatis, a French physician. Tomatis was the first to identify the different physiologies involved in listening and hearing. He also pioneered the concept that a baby can hear in utero. After his revolutionary work in the 1950s he had many followers and other researchers continue to develop his concepts. Today there are literally thousands of references and resources using music for therapeutic value.

Whatever your threshold, music can be hugely beneficial in organizing and calming your brain and has potential benefit for all of us. I elaborate on this important self-regulatory strategy in Chapter 7.

If your score on the Sensory Systems Checklist for auditory input was between -2 and -10, employ the following *avoiding* strategies to reduce auditory overload:

- Avoid noisy environments, busy malls, etc.
- Work flexi-time to avoid driving during peak traffic
- Commute by bus, sit at the back or right in front, put on your ear phones and relax
- Wear earplugs
- Put on your earphones and listen to calming music (this is sometimes not appropriate and practical in the work environment)
- Turn down the volume of your music, radio, TV, cellphone
- Close the door (hopefully you're not in an open-plan office)
- Carpets are noise reducing
- Offices can be set up with noise-reducing ceiling boards that facilitate draining of noise in a work environment
- Use white noise or calming, repetitive sounds to reduce the effect of distracting noises
- Use time-out or quiet times regularly (going to the bathroom is an excellent and appropriate excuse)
- Restrict noise during busy times. Switch off your cellphone and the TV when cooking dinner or bathing your children.

If your score on the Sensory Systems Checklist for auditory input was between +2 and +10, you possibly self-regulate effectively through the auditory system and the following auditory activities can be beneficial and should be part of your sensory diet:

- Music, music and more music
- Audio books
- Social gatherings and discussions
- Humming, whistling or singing
- Switching on the radio or TV
- Attending concerts and music shows
- Reading aloud.

The two hidden senses

We have touched on the two hidden senses, both related to movement, namely the vestibular and proprioceptive senses. Together these constitute the movement sensory system.

THE MOVEMENT SYSTEM

The sense of movement is described as the hidden sense of the body and brain. It is so automatic, occurring unconsciously, that we don't even think about it. Have you ever thought that the mere act of sitting up straight in your chair is a product of the receptors in your inner ear responding to gravity? While sitting, your brain is identifying the pull of gravity and aligning your body accordingly. Together with feedback from your joints and muscles you are maintaining your posture and tone unconsciously. Isn't that amazing!

It is important to distinguish between two different senses within the movement system. Whenever movement is generated, it is the product of two closely collaborating senses namely the *vestibular sense* and the *proprioceptive sense*.

The *vestibular* system is located in the inner ear, therefore you actually have a vestibular receptor in each ear. It responds whenever there is a change in head position, in other words whenever your head is turned or moved, the vestibular system is activated. The vestibular system also responds to gravity. It is quite appropriate to call the vestibular system your body's GPS (global position system). What a GPS does for a ship at sea, the vestibular system does for your body within your space. It gives the brain and body an idea where you are in space and how to orient yourself accordingly. The more jerky or the faster a movement is, for instance in a roller-coaster ride, the more the vestibular system is activated. Gymnastics, for instance, will stimulate the vestibular system much more than running or biking. Gymnastics routines involve rolling and tumbling which lead to many more changes in head position than simple forward motion.

The *proprioceptive* system is located in all your joints and muscles. There are receptors triggering a response to the brain whenever you move any muscle in your body. In a way it can be described as the 'body sense'. It gives you a reference point to where your body is in space (for instance your arms are up in the air), whereas the vestibular system tells you about your head position in space (for instance you are upside down). Climbing down stairs, walking to the bathroom at night without having to turn on the light, combing your hair, and millions more little physical actions you do daily are a product of the proprioceptive system.

There is a strong neurological link between the vestibular and proprioceptive systems and therefore they are grouped as the movement system. However, it is vital to distinguish between the two senses in the movement system because you can have a mixed pattern for thresholds. For instance, you can have a low threshold for vestibular input, meaning there is discomfort, nausea or avoidance with activities involving lots of head movement. Because of the link with the visual system, we find low vestibular threshold individuals are often fearful of heights. But they can have a typical or high threshold for proprioceptive input. This means that they can use the movement system to self-regulate by using muscles and joints, especially through resistance, but not where lots of head movement is involved.

Movement is a highly effective and universal regulator for the body and can be used successfully in stress management/ self-regulation. Low thresholds for proprioception seem fairly uncommon, although they do occur from time to time and have been documented in paediatric literature. I have not yet come across an adult with sensitivity for proprioception. Apart from the sensory pathways and connections within the part of your brain that makes you feel awake and alert, endorphins or happy hormones are released during exercise. The exercise industry is huge in promoting physical fitness for general well-being, and healthy control of stress. From a sensory perspective, the same truth applies. Each individual should choose the type of exercise (whether it be yoga or rock climbing) to suit his or her unique sensory needs and regulate the brain and body. This will be part of your sensory diet. I discuss sensory diets in depth in Chapter 6.

Living with movement

Your body physically takes you where you need to go as directed by your cortex and other brain structures. Although a subconscious part of functioning, you will find it difficult to participate in life if you are not physically active. If the brain is the orchestra, the movement system can be described as the conductor. This analogy comes close to illustrating the important role of the movement system in directing us within our environment. The skills of walking, coordinating movement and balancing the body are products of the movement system. Whenever you're walking, driving, sitting down, climbing stairs, using lifts or escalators, it is your movement system that silently helps your physical body to go through the motions without you even having to think about it.

Movement stressors (based on thresholds) are more prevalent in the vestibular system than in the proprioceptive system. Can you remember the last time your vestibular system failed you? When you experienced motion sickness (feeling air, car or sea sick), felt dizzy when getting up quickly (not due to blood pressure or low blood-glucose levels) or tripped over an object? Low thresholds for movement are why people avoid escalators and lifts – they experience discomfort with the movement. Many clients complain about being late for appointments because they use the stairs instead of the lift to get to the 13th floor of a building. It is certainly good from an exercise, movement self-regulation perspective, but may be somewhat embarrassing when you arrive at a meeting all sweaty and red in the face, gasping for breath before you manage to whisper a hoarse greeting. What if you need to be on the 22nd floor? But this is a reality; people with low thresholds for vestibular input avoid lifts and escalators as they feel uncomfortable and nauseous in a moving lift and the experience may trigger unnecessary anxiety.

A strong indicator of high vestibular thresholds is a love of carnival and roller-coaster rides, bungee jumping and other adrenaline driven sports. It is usually the vestibular sensation seekers who thrive on these activities; they get a kick out of activities such as these, feeding the sensory needs of their brains. In addition to the release of all the happy hormones, it is the success story people enjoy. If you have never experienced activities like these but desperately want to, you are probably a movement seeker with high thresholds. Then there are the others, like me, who get car sick, wouldn't dream of getting into a boat, wouldn't take a roller-coaster ride or bungee jump for all the money in the world. The mere thought is enough to send us into sensory overload and break out in a cold sweat. We have low thresholds for vestibular input. Although desensitization of the brain is possible across all the senses, motivation is the key. Even though I know very well that the concept of habituation includes the vestibular system and that if I do decide to go on 100 roller-coaster rides so that by number 101 my brain would say: "OK, I get it, I submit, I'll do it", I have absolutely no desire to go on 100 roller-coaster rides, so that by number 101 I would no longer feel nauseous. It's just not that important to me.

This brings us to a very important consideration: you sensory thresholds and resultant sensory preferences are a problem that needs to be addressed *only when they impact on your life negatively*. Motivation, wanting to change behaviours based on sensory needs because they affect your life adversely, is the key to intervention or change.

Case studies on movement stressors

Movement stressors can result in some irritation and discomfort especially with regard to using public transport, lifts, escalators and other moving objects. The movement sense does, however, seem to present the least amount of daily stressors for individuals. I've actually found that a lack of movement stimulation in people's sensory diet is a bigger problem. The movement system is a significant and powerful sensory self-regulator with huge benefits, which is not always understood and used to its full potential. Often the movement system is used to override and self-regulate defensive patterns in the other systems.

Ruth* is an active, 45-year old health professional with a sensation seeking profile. She is always busy, on the go, multi-tasking and enjoying a variation of activities, specifically in sport and recreation. She had to undergo a back operation and was basically on bed rest for six weeks. She found this extremely distressing because it was contradicting her sensory needs for movement and activity. During this time she became very depressed and irritable. Introducing activities in a prone position proved to be very challenging and somewhat fruitless. Although being on bed rest for six weeks would potentially be a difficult situation for most of us, Ruth found it especially difficult owing to her sensory profile and need for movement. She had to pace herself with extreme caution also after the six-week period to avoid introducing too much movement too soon.

Avoid or self-regulate through movement

Movement has extensive self-regulatory properties. It is often the best self-regulator and should therefore form part of your sensory diet. Bear in mind that both low and high threshold individuals for the movement system can use this sense to self-regulate.

Depending on your individual threshold, you should be able to identify whether you should use gentle, calmer movement (low thresholds) or fast, irregular and intense movement (high thresholds). If you have a low threshold for input from the vestibular system the following may lead to overload and should be avoided if possible:

- Activities with the head upside down, such as somersaults, cartwheels and roller-coaster rides
- Activities such as gymnastics, skydiving and bungee jumping
- Diving head-first off a diving board or a cliff into the water
- Elevators, escalators or high places.

Whether you choose solo sport or group activities will be determined by your touch, visual and auditory thresholds. Low threshold individuals for the touch, visual, smell and auditory systems would likely feel overwhelmed in groups of people moving, shouting, etc. Therefore, also consider your touch, visual and auditory thresholds when choosing a movement activity.

Many factors play a role when movement is used as a self-regulation tool. For this reason the following table is used to group movements according to their different sensory properties.

Controlled movement with minimal vestibular processing	Most suitable for low threshold movement profiles	Walking; Yoga; Pilates; Swinging in a hammock; Rocking in a rocking chair; Fishing; Road running
Activities with strong/heavy work input which increase proprioception – the universal modulator	Generally suitable for all profiles	Trail running; Biking; Canoeing; Mountain climbing; Tennis; Gym – weight training; Trampoline jumping; Hiking with a heavy backpack; Pushing a baby in a stroller; Taking a dog for a walk (the bigger the dog, the more the pull, the more proprioception!)
Busy movement with increased vestibular processing	Most suitable for high threshold movement profiles	Cricket, rugby, soccer; Parachuting, sky diving, hang gliding; Kite surfing; Surfing; Skiing (snow and water); Bungee jumping; Rock climbing; Gym – Aerobic exercises; White river rafting; Dancing; Rollerblading; Volley ball; Gymnastics; Polo; Yachting
Movement with added touch components	Suitable for mid-high thresholds for touch and movement	Swimming; Scuba diving; Wrestling; Karate; Boxing; Rugby; Contact sport

Watersports, particularly scuba diving and swimming, are generally very calming and soothing for individuals with a general sensory sensitive profile. They are very much calmed by experiencing a sense of a 'vacuum' under the water. Being underwater is a natural way to create a 'sensory deprivation chamber'. Your movement choice would also be affected by the following:

- Physical health. Always consult your physician regarding your general health before you commence an exercise regime
- Location and socio-economic status. People living in rural areas might not have access to the sea for diving or skiing and polo is something you've only seen on a shirt, a very expensive one. Your socio-economic status would influence your choice, as would the availability of movement activities such as paragliding, yachting, and going to the gym versus walking, biking and walking stairs. The bottom line is, everyone can move!

MULTI-SENSORY COMBINATIONS: ACTIVITY LEVEL

Activity level refers to our active involvement in daily routines. Activities are predominantly performed in the area of work, play and self-care. The activities we are involved in are dependent on our age, sex, life roles and cycles, culture and health status.

Living with activity

Our daily activities in life are a multi-sensory process because we have to use a combination of our senses to perceive what is happening and what we should do next. I believe that mothers in general, especially working mothers, need to function by multi-tasking 99% of the time. Dealing with the demands of a relationship, raising children, running a home and in most instances holding down a job as well, requires meticulous timing, planning and organization. Whatever and wherever you are in life, there is a demand from your environment and your life to act. That means using your hands, feet, ears, eyes, mouth, nose and skin and getting going. We do not live, nor operate, in a vacuum. Considering the high, multi-sensory demands of every day living, it is important to take a break from time to time. Go away for a weekend, or even just a day. *TAKE FIVE, TAKE A BREAK*; it is vital to catch your breath and recharge.

Case studies on activity stressors

It is very interesting to note the level of activity within different sensory profiles. There are definite trends in sensory profiles with regard to activity level, mostly that low threshold people want less whereas high threshold people want more. This factor certainly contributes to forming and moulding the type, intensity and frequency of activities in our lives. The stressors below are, however, evident in both low and high threshold individuals:

- Organizing work, homes, lives
- Managing time effectively
- Getting up in the morning
- Falling asleep at night
- Concentration, attention and focus
- Stress management.

Nadia* is a 44-year old woman who lives in a rural town close to Cape Town. She has a long history of regular job changes. She started off studying drama then switched to law, which was interrupted a few times but eventually she finished her law degree. She often moved and often changed jobs, trying to find a place where she felt she could belong. When in a job situation, she performs well and gives her best but she cannot sustain it. Living in the country suits her sensory profile, but she needs to hold down a job to earn a living. She describes the situation thus: "My health and my career don't go together; it's too stressful but I don't know how to approach it." She says: "I find life too busy around me, too much noise and movement, in short – I find life and being involved in society ('normal life') too exhausting. Too many thoughts in my head and too little time to deal with them. Outside influences (i.e. people, traffic) exhaust me." Nadia has high levels of anxiety and often feels depressed. She struggles to make decisions, she calls her brain 'scrambled', wanting to build a lifestyle but feeling unable to cope with all the sensory overload around her. She is an extrovert who loves people but at the same time finds them too exhausting owing to her sensitivity. She has a significantly sensory defensive profile with severe sensitivity for tactile, auditory, and visual input, mild sensitivity for taste and smell input and normal thresholds for movement. Her activity levels fluctuate significantly throughout the day. She really battles to get out of bed in the morning, only starting to function at about 10. Then she struggles to fall asleep at night. She has a disorganized 'busy-ness' that often leads to more overload. She often goes into sensory shutdown, literally withdrawing from the world and closing herself up in her own home. Gaining insight into and understanding of her sensory world and needs was a huge and positive process for Nadia and following the correct sensory diet and brushing therapy, helped her to start coping with life's demands.

Avoid or self-regulate through activities

Bear in mind the general rule: low threshold profiles (sensory sensitives and/or sensation avoiders) usually need fewer activities whereas high threshold profiles (low registrators and/or sensation seekers) need more activities.

If your score on the Sensory Systems Checklist for activity level was between -2 and -10, you should employ *avoiding* strategies to reduce sensory overload:

- Maintain routines, consistency and predictability
- Familiarity of people, settings and experiences would be safer and more manageable (i.e. always going to the same restaurant)
- Spend more time in nature (hiking, fishing, boating, etc.)
- Use regular breaks and time-out
- Create 'womb spaces' for calming and organizing the senses
- Give yourself permission and opportunities to be alone
- Sequence and organize your world
- Plan and organize activities well before doing them
- Avoid crowds, traffic, congested areas
- Meditation and/or relaxing activities are crucial
- Follow a regular exercise program ('quiet', solo activities are ideal).

If your score on the Sensory Systems Checklist for activity level was between +2 and +10, you possibly self-regulate effectively through activities and the following would probably be beneficial and should be part of your sensory diet:

- Participate in group activities
- Incorporate novelty and variety in your daily routines at work and at home
- Find new ways to do old things (for instance, take a different route to work)
- Introduce new people, settings and experiences into your life
- Incorporate change regularly (move furniture in your home, take on a new project, etc.)

- Offer to organize the office Christmas party, your child's school play, etc.
- Regularly invite friends over
- Go to plays, concerts, movies, exhibitions, etc.
- Follow a regular exercise program (multi-sensory group activities are ideal).

If your score on the Sensory Systems Checklist for any system was -1, 0 or +1 you are possibly neither sensitive nor seeking for that system which can be considered to have normal thresholds. Such systems are mostly balanced and accessible.

Summary of the senses

Our brains are constantly receiving information from all our senses. Some information is unimportant and the brain habituates and let it go. Other information is important; the brain sensitizes and we orient and attend to it. This mixing and matching of millions of sensory inputs occurring all the time creates a massive traffic flow in our brains. Some of us have some congestion in some areas, a few crashes, others drive too fast and others too slow. Every brain is unique but the bottom line is that the modulation and regulation of all the senses together help us pay attention, focus, learn, work, perform, interact with other people, interact with the environment and live life. Looking at the brain and body from this primitive level it is therefore natural for us to conclude that the following are all products of proper sensory modulation and integration:

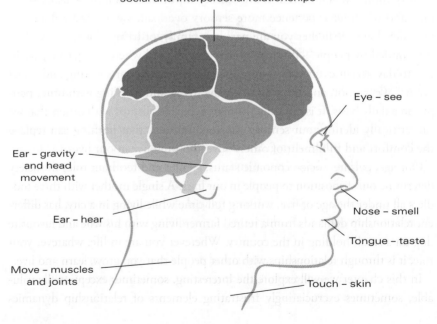

Executive functions – thoughts, abstract reasoning, actions, performance, social and interpersonal relationships

Eye – see

Ear – gravity – and head movement

Ear – hear

Nose – smell

Tongue – taste

Move – muscles and joints

Touch – skin

To my sons, Lukas and Henrick,
Thank you for sharing me with my work. I love you!

CHAPTER 4

Sensory intelligent relationships

We live in a sensory world where our brains and bodies are continuously and consistently bombarded by what is happening in the environment. Those lucky enough to live and work in a quiet and secluded environment constitute a small percentage of society. Certain cultures separate themselves from the rest of the world and sometimes one cannot help wishing for something similar.

We are also constantly surrounded by people. If you are part of a family, this usually includes a spouse, children, siblings, grandmothers, grandfathers, the list is endless. Then add the family cat or dog, and no one will blame us if we sometimes feel like we're living in a zoo. Where there are people there is more sensory input. When there is more sensory input, there is more sensory overload and when we experience more sensory overload, we get stressed and go into shutdown. Whether you are part of a family, or living alone, you will be surrounded by people – if not at home, at work and where you participate in day to day activities such as shopping, running chores, or sporting and social events. We cannot, and should not escape living and working with other people on a daily basis. It is not only through our relationships with others that we can critically identify our sensory stressors, but also that nothing can replace the comfort and fulfilment of others' love and presence in our lives.

Our age, culture, socio-economic status, gender and resultant roles in society determine our disposition to people in our lives. A single mother with three toddlers all under the age of five, working full-time while living in a city, has different relationship demands from a retired farmer living with his wife and favourite dog on a small-holding in the country. Wherever you are in life, whatever your role, it is through relationships with other people that you grow, learn and live.

In this chapter we will explore the interesting, sometimes exceptionally valuable, sometimes excruciatingly frustrating elements of relationship dynamics based on sensory profiles. In my experience so far, an insight into and understanding of relationship dynamics from a sensory perspective has been extremely useful, often changing people's lives and attitudes 180°. When conflict in our relationships is analysed and identified as being caused by 'sensory irritations', which are completely manageable, we move away from negative emotions towards an understanding of one another on a new level. Understanding brings acceptance and conflict resolution. We drop labels, stop blaming ourselves and others, and accept ourselves and others for who we are, able to enjoy life, whether we are overloaded or underloaded by the world around us.

The sensory tree

When developing my application of sensory intelligence I had to find a way to make the concept come alive. Pictures have always been a successful medium to explain and teach new concepts. That is when I came up with my *Sensory tree,* a simple, effective way to explain sensory intelligent relationships. A tree typically has deep roots, reaching down into the soil for life-giving nutrients deep in the earth, surface roots that help anchor it, a trunk, and branches covered in leaves, reaching out for the life-giving warmth of the sun.

Sensation avoiders

Sensation avoiders

People with sensation avoiding profiles are like the deep, anchoring roots of a tree; they like it dark, comfortable and cosy with an abundance of peace and quiet. Not much is going on deep under the earth. Sensation avoiders typically need more quiet space, clear expectations and prefer predictable rituals. But they are like roots in other ways as well; they are solid and steadfast people who anchor others, families, organizations, etc. They provide structure, predictability and make sure that this growing organism is fed so that it can grow. They constitute the foundation that is crucial to maintain growth and prevent the tree from dying or toppling over.

Sensation seekers

Sensation seekers, on the other hand are like the leaves of a tree. They grow, change colour, move in the wind, attract attention with the butterflies, the bees and the birds. They get sunlight, rain, hail, wind and whatever nature sends their way. They are the clear, visible signs that the tree is growing. Sensation seekers as the leaves are always ready for something new and unpredictable, ready to change and grow with new ideas and components, sometimes wild and colourful. They need activity, variety, novelty and enjoy change.

Typical thresholds

Those of us with typical thresholds (neither low nor high thresholds) can be described as the trunk of the tree – the icing in the Oreo cookie, the glue that keeps things together. If you are a trunk rather than roots or leaves, you probably had difficulty working through the assessment chapter and might have thought that you were 'too boring' or 'too normal'. Surprisingly, based on my preliminary pilot studies using the sensory profile, only 18,5% of people tested fell within normal/typical thresholds. An interesting observation is that all these people described themselves as easy going, even-tempered, are often used as negotiators, and usually cope well in all kinds of life situations. Individuals with this type of profile usually find it easy to adapt to either avoiders or seekers. For this reason I call them the 'icing in the oreo cookie' – they are the glue that keeps people, organizations, societies and families together with relative ease.

Low registrators and sensory sensitives

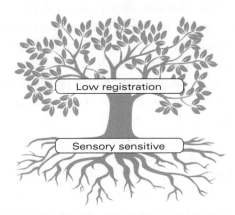

Low registrators are like the branches of the tree. They are on the high threshold spectrum but more passively inclined. They can be dreamers, yet conscientious, easily performing their tasks and duties without experiencing disruption from other sensory input. Like branches they are steady and supply another important backbone. They transfer the food they receive from the roots via the trunk to the leaves to energize them for their sensation seeking dance in the wind.

Sensory sensitives are like the surface roots of the tree. They are on the low threshold spectrum; they are sensitive to and aware of the environment, but they are also more passively inclined.

They are acutely aware of their sensory environment but do not over-respond actively by reaching down into the soil. They are therefore inclined to be more tolerant of busy environments for longer periods of time than sensation avoiders. But they carry the same rooting traits; they prefer quietness, peace and calm but do not necessarily seek this out actively.

Complete interdependence

If we look at the two extremes of deep roots and leaves we identify two absolute opposites in sensory profiles, in managing life, tasks and people. But while these two profiles are so different and their co-existence often the cause of much friction and conflict, the bottom line is that they need one another in order to grow. They also need the 'in-between' profiles to help them connect, to nurture them, to stabilize them.

Considering that there are five different sensory profiles, with a large degree of possible mixture of patterns, different styles, different needs, different behaviours, it is obvious that conflict will arise, especially where people with opposite profiles co-exist. However, diversity to any degree is crucial in sustaining relationships and growth in whatever life situation we may find ourselves. Exploring the conflicts between profiles will increase insight, facilitate acceptance and help us realize that other people do not necessarily experience the world in the same way we do. I believe the acceptance of harmony and diversity between different profiles can be most beneficial in growing relationships at home and at work.

Goodness of fit

Goodness of fit in this context refers to how people (and their resultant relationships) relate to one another to produce a positive or negative outcome. Obviously we always aim for achieving an optimal goodness of fit. That would mean that people are suited to one another, to their environments and to their life demands.

Here we will explore primarily the goodness of fit between individuals and look at relationships between partners, parents and children, and siblings.

Although goodness of fit is particularly relevant and useful when considering the relationships between people, the relationship between individuals and their particular environment is another important factor to consider. We create happier relationships when understanding the goodness of fit dynamics between us and the people within our world. When we understand our and their sensory needs we can be more accommodating and accepting. When we identify our own sensory needs and apply that to the environments where we live and operate, it is another powerful tool in creating the best, most productive place for us to live and work.

I have seen many clients suddenly expand their horizons, finding peace and happiness, when achieving a perfect or near perfect goodness of fit between their sensory needs and their environment. Environment in this context refers to the sensory properties of that physical area. For instance, the optimal environment for someone who has low thresholds, whose sensory needs indicate less input, would be a home which is clean, structured, organized, has gentle lighting with reduced noise. Looking beyond the properties of the immediate environment, it would be ideal if the house is in a quiet street overlooking a park rather than on a busy corner opposite a preschool. Furthermore, this person would need a quiet space within her home where she can relax, unwind and de-stress. A work environment for the low threshold person should ideally be contained, structured and predictable but still enhance her sense of creativity and inventiveness.

Goodness of fit is dealt with more extensively in Chapter 7 and work-related relationships and goodness of fit between colleagues and environments are discussed in Chapter 8.

GOODNESS OF FIT IN RELATIONSHIPS

This discussion of the relationship dynamics between different profiles will provide you with the necessary information to determine your unique pattern within your chosen relationships. Both negative and positive elements will be highlighted. It is important to identify stressors coming from the people in your life (often indicating the negative elements) as this creates unnecessary conflict. Once you understand that these behaviours have a primitive, sensory origin, rather than being wilful or conscious, you can become more accepting, supportive and loving. The positive elements should then be reinforced to make your relationship special and unique. We help and support one another through our diversity, and fill the gaps where our partners might fail.

Goodness of fit in relationships includes fit between partners, spouses, parents and children, siblings, teachers and children, colleagues, friends, employees and employers. There are obviously many more, but I will focus mainly on two main relationship dynamics, namely between partners, and between parents and children. But the principles can be applied to any relationship you wish to explore. I chose this focus based on my clinical exposure and related case studies. Also, most people have a partner at some point in time. Some for shorter periods than others, but it is often through our partner relationships that we grow and are challenged. Relationships are complicated and need time, energy and input. The better we know, understand, accept and nurture our partners, the more peace, love and harmony we will experience.

The relationship between parents and children is of particular interest to me since this has been my clinical focus for so many years. As parents we have a very important role to educate, lead and prepare our children for the future. On a sensory level we are responsible for the stimulation of our children for optimal growth and development. It is through sensory exploration that children experience and learn about their world. When we know our children's sensory needs, as well as our own, we are better equipped to optimize their learning environment without under- or over-stimulating them, both of which extremes may be detrimental to children's development on a sensory, motor and social level. If we strive and work towards providing a balanced environment we can raise children with a strong self-belief and confidence, contributing to their becoming happy, positive and successful individuals.

Getting back to goodness of fit, although there are many variables in individual profiles, I will mostly refer to the main categories of sensation seekers and sensation avoiders. Since they have the active profiles, they often experience more conflict and therefore also benefit more from addressing the reasons for these conflicts. The passive profiles will be discussed briefly after the main categories.

Bear in mind that active profiles try to counteract the nervous system threshold and would introduce or avoid activities to fit their sensory needs. The passive profiles (low registrators and sensory sensitives) are as important. They act in accordance with their thresholds and do not employ actions to introduce or avoid activities to fit their sensory needs.

A general truth for the main profile categories is that leaves/sensation seekers (high thresholds) need *more* and roots/sensation avoiders (low thresholds) need *less*. More and less here refer to sensory input. I guess one could say that for roots *less is more* and for leaves *more is more*.

Partners/spouses relationship dynamics

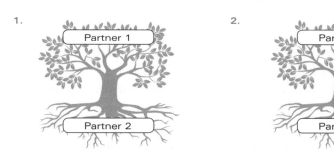

Harmony/Benefit

The leaves will be creating more sensory input, be more active, more inclined and willing to undertake activities, social gatherings and enjoy bright and lively environments where a lot of people are present. They will be challenging the roots to be more sociable, to participate in more activities and to explore more. The roots are the stability elements, creating a sense of calm and peace by reducing sensory input and making time to just be together without too much activity and/or people. Roots have a calming effect on leaves. We know that opposites attract!

Conflict

Since the sensory needs of roots and leaves are so different, their respective pursuit and avoidance of sensation can create a lot of friction, irritation and conflict. Leaves want to go out, roots want to stay home. Leaves want to go to a new restaurant, roots prefer the tried and tested restaurant, as they know the food and environment and feel safer. Leaves can be overpowering and 'too much' for the roots, because they are often too busy, too loud, too talkative, etc., and create sensory overload for the roots. Sensory overload leads to the brain and body going into stress, often with negative results. Roots, on the other hand, can be too withdrawn, too controlling and too predictable.

Goodness of fit verdict

YES. Although you will experience much diversity and conflict, you will be challenging each other positively as well. You will complete one another. A good sense of balance between your profiles can be obtained with insight, compassion and understanding for each other. Handle the conflicts positively and appreciate the differences.

3.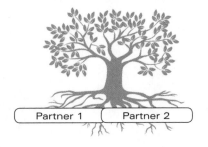

Partner 1 | Partner 2

Harmony/Benefit

Your sensory needs are similar. You would rather stay at home and listen to your favourite music or read a book rather than go out. You are both calm, peaceful and reduce the amount of sensory input within your lives. Your home is your secure space and you often understand each other without even talking. You enjoy quiet time together and find your activities harmonizing readily.

Conflict

You both are inclined to be structured, rigid and controlling. You can be set in your ways and then not willing to compromise on your routines, likes or dislikes. You must guard against withdrawing too much from society or not exploring new avenues, new activities and new people.

Goodness of fit verdict

YES. You are a compatible couple with similar sensory needs. You would potentially be drawn to the same activities and environments and possibly even chose the same décor for your home.

4.

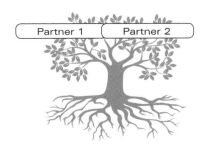

Harmony/Benefit

You are crazy together. You share a zest for life, engaging in fun, frantic, wild activities together and always have sufficient energy left to be further challenged. You are the couple who may go skydiving or kite-surfing together. You energize and challenge each other. You often operate and think similarly and would stretch each other's boundaries without even noticing it or experiencing discomfort. You probably enjoy socializing and have a wide circle of friends. You always get invited to all the parties.

Conflict

You are inclined to take activities too far, not always knowing when to stop, when to rest and when to slow down. You may be draining and exhausting each other and you both may only realize that when it's too late. You can create more stress within your home or life structures by being too busy or adding too much. You often have too many obligations and responsibilities. You have too little quiet or away time.

Goodness of fit verdict

YES. You are a well-matched couple. You will have loads of fun with similar interests and activities. Just try to be more in tune with your bodies so that you can assist each other when the going gets tough. It is okay to stop, rest and take time out occasionally.

Parent-child relationship dynamics

We will once again focus on the active profiles, but do bear in mind that you or your child may also be a low registrator or sensory sensitive. Important facts to consider are that low registrators have a tendency to miss information in their environments. They can be dreamy or 'in a world of their own', which can make it difficult to reach them or get them to pay attention to their environment. They are good at caring for crying babies and noisy toddlers as their systems do not seem to get overloaded so quickly. Sensory sensitives are in tune with the environment and often in touch with their partners and children. They are caring and supportive, but may experience sensory overload with sustained input, activities or demands.

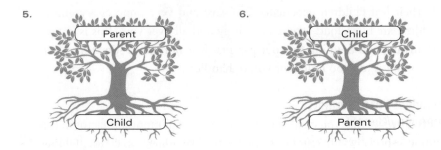

Harmony/Benefit

Leaves and roots challenge each other, and for children with growing, developing and maturing brains this is extremely important. In scenario 5 the parent will provide stimulation for the child, exposing him to different activities and environments which the child may not initiate or seek out. For example the parent may include the child in shopping activities or encourage participation in a peer-group activity. The child will have a calming effect on the parent, creating or forcing time out and being alone with the parent. In scenario 6 the child will seek the stimulation and create sensory input leaving the parent to simply facilitate activities. For example the child will beg the parent to take him to an amusement park or busy area, which forces the parent to step out of a quiet, comfortable zone and participate in activities with the child. The parent will create structure and routine in the child's life. From a challenge perspective these profiles work well.

Conflict

Unfortunately both profile dynamics create excessive conflict as the chances of the leaf overloading the root are frequent and intense. Parents in scenario 5 should not expose their children to too many activities, crowds, clutter and stuff. You are important in facilitating new learning opportunities, but be aware of the fact that you can overload your child very quickly and then often be confronted with negative, unpredictable and uncontrolled behaviour. Bear in mind that children's nervous and sensory systems are immature and that they cannot control them as well as adults do, or hope to. Children under 10 in particular may still show unpredictable and explosive behaviours because some of the pathways in the brain between the cortex (thinking and managing brain) and the limbic (emotional brain) system have not yet fully developed. Remember with roots, less is more. Yes, do expose your child, gently in a positive encouraging manner to participate, but if you are too pushy you are likely to send him over the edge leaving you with negative and undesirable outcomes.

Parents in scenario 6 often complain that their children are just way too much for them. I have seen parents who really battle to cope with and handle their leaf children experience excessive and very unnecessary guilt. Leaf children are busy, loud, exuberant, lively and all over you. This is potentially exhausting and draining for root parents. It is normal to sometimes feel that your child is just too much for you to handle.

Goodness of fit verdict

YES. The fact that you challenge one another is an important factor in this dynamic, especially with regard to enhancing development in children. However, the conflict potential in this dynamic is real and extensive. Loads of patience, understanding and strategies are necessary to harness positive emotions and energy.

 7.

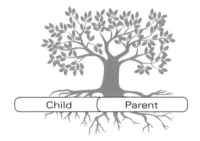

Harmony/Benefit

There is a sense of calm and contentedness between this child and parent. They would be very happy cuddling in front of the TV, watching their favourite nature programme. The sensory needs of a child and a parent who are both roots are similar – less is more, quiet is good and being in their own environment is preferred. I guess this parent and child would potentially be very much in tune with each other, their needs, wants and stressors. Conversation and sharing may be optimal and easily obtained. Do not think that only quiet activities would be preferred. Outdoor sport and activity would be based around playing cricket in the garden, going for a walk in a forest or riding bikes.

Conflict

These profiles show a hermit tendency and often isolate themselves from the world to an extent. During my years of paediatric practice I often came across this as a potential problem, as root parents tend to be overprotective and if they have root children, withhold the necessary sensory play and experiences from them, like playing in the mud, messing with food (babies, not five-year olds), water play, etc. These are the parents who are obsessive about cleaning their children, wiping hands and faces and thereby depriving their children of sensory input. Being dirty and messing around with clay, paint, mud, water are vital sensory learning opportunities for children and a crucial part of their normal development. This child may not want to go to a birthday party and the parent will much rather keep him at home than going accompanying him to a noisy, busy, normal gathering of running, screaming, shouting five-year-olds. I'm referring to a typical fourth of fifth birthday party of a boy. If you are a root, you'll know exactly how much sensory overload I'm talking about. But it is through exposure that we help our children to get de-sensitized and more comfortable in multi-sensory environments. Root children potentially avoid many things (new clothing, soaps, sock seams, cutting nails, washing and brushing hair, etc.), but it is through gentle exposure and encouragement that we help them cope better with the normal sensory demands of life.

Goodness of fit verdict

YES. But be sure to make a special effort to stimulate and challenge your children. Thereby you will be effectively expanding your own sensory thresholds too. Root parents should also guard against over-protecting their children. We need to protect our children yes, but they also need a certain level of safe exploration.

8.

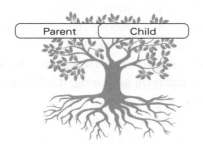

Harmony/Benefit

Here's the crazy couple again. This parent and child will engage in many different types of activities and games. Together they are busy, lively and on the go, forever rushing off to the next activity. Their sensory need for 'more' drives them and they would be the ones enjoying a raucous birthday party for five-year-olds, going to a shopping centre during peak hours, visiting museums, parks and play areas at all times of the day. They energize one another and feed off each other's need for activity and sensory input, rarely getting tired. They thrive on new activities, surprises and people.

Conflict

Too much of a good thing is never good. Knowing when to stop, rest and take a break is often difficult for these profiles. Especially for children, parents need to enforce structure, discipline and routine on a daily basis. This helps them learn to plan, organize and manage their world. Following rules, respecting boundaries and operating within set structures are often difficult for leaves and they need to make a special effort to acquire and implement these important life skills.

Goodness of fit verdict

YES. Have fun! But do stop occasionally, take a break and rest!

9.

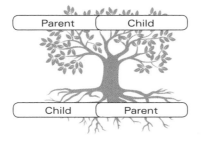

This profile distribution is not that common, but remains relevant. This refers to changing or fluctuating thresholds for parents and children. Some profiles have both seeking and avoiding traits, which complicates relationships and coping dynamics, because of the sudden changes and unpredictability of be-haviours and stressors. Bear in mind that these fluctuations of thresholds often refer to different systems, namely being a sensation seeker for movement, but a sensation avoider for auditory input/hearing. Read Chapter 3 again for details on the different systems.

Harmony/Benefit

Owing to different threshold patterns these profiles can shift to the other end easily. When needing to cope with a noisy, loud and unpredictable environ-ment they can shift to accommodate those elements within the environment without being overloaded, irritated and experiencing discomfort. For parents it can be beneficial as it helps them cope with their children in different states.

Conflict

There is considerable unpredictability and sudden changes in how profiles react to the environment and people. Conflict is relevant and real owing to different needs at different times. A child with fluctuating thresholds might be needing quietness and predictability in one situation but the complete opposite in another situation. It makes the management of a relationship a hit-and-miss affair, as we are often unsure what is going on.

Goodness of fit verdict

YES, maybe. At least life is never boring here, however tiring. I believe self-care and loads of patience are crucial.

General guidelines for healthy relationships

My apologies to readers who are currently parenting teenagers as the strategies suggested below are more relevant for ages from around three to ten. My exposure to and experience of working with adolescents have been rather limited and I feel ill equipped to give you specific guidelines. However, sensory needs remain sensory needs throughout, so be creative and apply the same principles in your relationship with your teenager. I guess more patience, love and holding one's tongue are required when dealing with this group of interesting creatures. I have a few years grace before being thrown in at the deep end with my own two boys.

For sensory management of babies in particular, please read *Baby sense* by Megan Faure and Ann Richardson (see References page 191). It is a wonderful source for guiding you towards a happy and contented baby.

Parenting a deep root (sensation avoider)
- Honour the need for space and time-out
- Create womb spaces (a hide-away quiet space) – use this when your child is overwrought, unmanageable or emotional and teach him to use it as a valuable coping strategy
- Structure time-out daily
- Prepare the child prior to new activities/situations
- Create structure and routine
- Use calming sensory input (Chapter 6)
- Use rigidity positively
- Talk (whisper) and have fun with your child
- Don't expose your child to large group activities unnecessarily
- Give fewer and quiet instructions.

Parenting a surface root (sensory sensitive)

- Allow for sensitivities without criticism
- Understand sensitivities to be real
- Create structure and routine
- Organize room and home spaces
- Use calming sensory input (Chapter 6)
- Use gentle persuasion to try new things
- Identify your child's keen awareness of the environment and detail
- Talk (softly) and have fun with your child
- Don't force your child to do things he is sensitive for
- Don't overload your child with multi-sensory input
- Limit extra mural activities.

Parenting a leaf (sensation seeker)

- Be creative and find interesting activities for your child to do
- Run/walk/move with your child
- Add variety and novelty on a regular basis
- Use colours and textures extensively
- Identify interesting and fun projects in and around the house
- Instil a sense of safety and caution
- Identify and provide creative outlets
- Talk (more) and have fun with your child
- Don't allow chaos and clutter
- Don't restrict movement activities
- Don't allow destructive energy.

Parenting a branch (low registrator)

- Look at and even hold your child when talking to him
- Give instructions only when you know your child is listening to you (make eye contact)
- Work according to a clock/watch
- Have clear and colourful lists of tasks/chores
- Give lots of feedback and cues
- Encourage group interactions
- Increase intensity of sensory input
- Use alerting sensory input (Chapter 6)
- Talk (louder) and have fun with your child
- Restrict TV and sedentary activities
- Reinforce active rather than passive play.

Partner of a deep root (sensation avoiders)

- Remember, they keep your feet on the ground
- Honour their need for space and time-out
- Approach them from the front, never sneak up on them from behind
- Work with their structure and routines, you might learn a few tricks
- Prepare them prior to introducing new activities/situations, never throw them a surprise party or tell them that something needs to be done at the last minute
- Touch them hard, firmly and don't tickle or stroke them softly
- They will like your deep hugs, but wipe off your soft kiss
- Talk softly, gently, never scream or yell
- Be calm and contented with them
- Don't force them into large group activities; they won't enjoy them and will be miserable anyway
- Find and tune into their self-regulatory activities and participate with them (solo sport, cooking, TV, reading, dancing)
- Tell them and show them that you love them.

Partner of a surface root (sensory sensitives)

- Remember they are in tune with you and the environment
- Allow for their sensitivities without criticism
- Create structure, order and routine
- Organize rooms and home spaces, be sure to de-clutter
- Use calming sensory input: softer, gentler, quieter, slower
- Ask them nicely with gentle persuasion to try new things
- Involve them in novel and new activities or people, but don't push it; once a week may be enough
- Acknowledge their keen awareness to the environment and detail
- Have gentle conversations, no screaming, yelling or criticizing
- Find and tune into their self-regulatory activities and participate with them (sport, dancing, art, pottery)
- Tell them and show them that you love them.

Partner of a leaf (sensation seekers)

- Remember they create change, new opportunities and broaden our horizons
- Be creative and find interesting activities to do
- Run/walk/move with them
- Add variety and novelty on a regular basis (re-arrange furniture, buy them new clothes, perfume, flowers, cook them interesting and flavour filled meals)
- Take them to a new restaurant, show, concert
- Throw them a surprise party, or surprise them with a new book, CD, picnic, etc.
- Talk to them, sing with them, listen to music with them
- Don't restrict them when they want to try something new
- Encourage group activities as the increased sensory input works for them – invite lots of people over
- Alert them to danger and safety issues
- Find their self-regulatory system activities and participate with them (sport, dancing, biking, bungee jumping, river rafting)
- Tell them and show them that you love them.

Partner of a branch (low registrator)

- Remember, they can hang in there and hang on forever
- Make eye contact before you talk to them, otherwise you might not get a response
- Help them to maintain a diary and work according to time and a clock or watch
- Give them colourful lists of tasks or chores in central places so that they can remember to do them
- Give them lots of feedback and cues
- Remind them about important meetings
- Encourage group activities as the increased sensory input works for them – invite several people over
- Talk louder, be energetic, give them hugs
- Have fun with them
- Find their self-regulatory system activities and participate with them (sport, music, dancing, pottery)
- Tell them and show them that you love them.

Chapters 5 and 7 will give you further insight into and strategies for coping with sensory overload, the key to a healthy relationship across profiles.

Relationship dynamics in case studies

John* is a 41 year old divorced executive living with his girlfriend Sally. They have difficulty managing conflict and feel that they are often 'on each other's cases'. After a series of conflict management sessions the therapist working with them referred them to me as she felt there was 'something sensory' going on. John has a strong sensation avoiding profile with significant tactile defensiveness. He has a tough job, is extremely successful, but often controlling and demanding of his staff. When he gets home in the afternoon he is tired, irritated and in total sensory overload. Sally, who has the exact same profile, comes home in the afternoon after a boring day at work and wants to spend time with him. This is often a time where irritations start to boil over and eventually lead to conflict and fights. Identifying and managing sensory overload was a crucial step for them in identifying each other's state of overload and how to cope with it. Some of the strategies were as simple as John going for a game of squash or to gym straight after work to help him release his tension and overload. When he got home after that, he felt more at ease and found he could relate more readily to Sally's needs. Identifying sensory overload and giving each other space during these times were crucial. John's avoidance of touching Sally was also misinterpreted as rejection. When she understood the origin of his withdrawal, she identified ways and times to introduce physical contact with him when his sensory system could tolerate it.

Anna* the 44-year old woman, living at home with her husband, has two children who have left home and live on their own. She describes herself as a difficult, fussy person who tends to be introspective. She enjoys social contact with people, but wants to be in control and the people and situations should be predictable. She avoids touch from others, prefers soft textures for clothing and blankets, always takes her shoes off and does not cook regularly as she hates having her hands dirty. She is a perfectionist who likes to control her world and her house is super tidy and clean. Anna has a significant sensory defensive (extreme sensitive) profile with sensitivity in most of her systems; she is a deep root. She was horrified when she identified her perfectionist behaviours with regards to cleaning her children when they were young. "I was always walking around with a wet cloth, cleaning their hands and faces". But I believe in focusing on the positive aspect of our sensory profiles. In our discussion it became evident that as her children grew up, Anna remained very much in tune with them as teenagers. "When they got home after a night out, I knew exactly whether they drank or smoked; what they drank or what they smoked." Her sensory defensive behaviours proved to be worthwhile in allowing her to be 100% in tune with her children. What is important is that you manage these intuitive behaviours towards your children and loved ones positively, guarding against being over-bearing and over-protecting.

Sharon* is 34 years old and has two toddlers of five and two years old. Her husband is a chef and runs a well-known restaurant in a big city. Sharon's five-year-old boy saw a colleague of mine for occupational therapy, and my colleague referred Sharon to me when she identified Sharon's difficulty in coping with her children. Sharon has a significant sensory avoidance profile with mostly visual and tactile sensitivity. She hates being dirty, always felt sticky when she was out in a shop or doing errands. She also couldn't sleep unless she had a shower at night. She did not enjoy being close to others, preferred small, familiar groups of people and would withdraw in social settings. She constantly felt overloaded by her children and unable to take some quiet time for herself. She loved escaping to her computer and could sit for hours working in this closed-off space. Because of her husband's long hours at the restaurant, Sharon had to run their household and care for the children mostly on her own. She felt very guilty about the fact that she just couldn't manage her children and felt totally drained by them. Insight into and awareness of her profile and the reason for her overload brought Sharon immense relief. Allowing herself quiet-time without feeling guilty, and getting help from a full time nanny were some of the strategies we implemented to help her cope.

Didi*, the 36 year old advocate, with a significant sensory defensive profile (also mentioned in Chapter 3) was married to a rock musician. Their sensory incompatibility, together with other factors contributed to a break down in their marriage, which resulted in divorce. After Didi started working with me she managed to identify the sensory origin of many of their conflict issues. I believe that with insight, understanding and the right strategies, any relationship can work. Didi also struggles with her lively and noisy little three-year-old daughter. "My noise sensitivity creates great tension between my little girl and myself. I get jumpy and cranky when she does the normal three year-old things such as shouting, dropping things, banging doors, etc. Sometimes I shout at her to stop. My daughter suffers because I nag and shout at her not to make a noise." Although Didi moved to a home office environment for doing her admin and case preparation she had to travel to the city for the actual court cases. She felt drained returning home afterwards. I suggested to Didi that she should join her daughter for a floor time play session every day as soon as she got back from work for only 20 minutes. During this time I asked her to give full, undivided attention to her daughter, not answering any phone calls or doing any chores. She should join her daughter playing with what her daughter wants to play with. Didi looked doubtful that this would make any difference, but I literally dared her to introduce this amazingly simple yet powerful strategy. Didi admitted to me afterwards that she thought I was crazy, but decided to give it a try. She was amazed and relieved at the results. Within days, after the 20 minutes of play, Didi was left to attend to dinner, chores, phone calls, etc., with her daughter happily playing in the background, not nagging or constantly demanding attention.

When I worked with Andrea*, her husband Ben* came to the helpful realization that 'the trip of a lifetime' he planned for himself and Andrea to the Amazon would not thrill her at all. Andrea, a sensory root, with her sensory sensitivity was overcome with nausea just thinking about slimy creatures and sticky, wet leaves touching her body. Ben, a sensory leaf, thought it would be an exciting adventure. By gaining insight into one another's sensory profiles they were able to make their decisions about holiday destinations without emotional responses and labelling. It helped them to know what the other needed and how to choose a place that would satisfy both their needs, while also allowing them to spend quality time together. Andrea also gave Ben the thumbs-up to do his Amazon trip with his brother or buddies.

I am currently working with Nina* and John* a couple who have been on the brink of divorce quite a few times over the last year. Nina is tactile defensive; she hates being touched, and remembers also as a child that she used to distance herself from others. She doesn't wear make up or polo necks, hates face cloths, calls herself a clean freak, she hates touching or brushing her hair and showers/baths twice a day. She is a rigid follower of routines and needs control in order to feel safe. Nina is obviously a deep root. John, on the other hand is a branch. While not quite a leaf, he has high thresholds, likes to socialize and going to new places all the time. The intimacy in their marriage took a serious dip owing to Nina's physical withdrawal. As the conflict and issues escalated, Nina withdrew more and more, tending to go into shutdown. John started to feel rejected by and angry with Nina, casting unnecessary blame. Since they began working with me, their understanding of and insight into their diverse sensory profiles have brought about a huge shift in their approach to their relationship as they are making allowances for each other's needs. Slowly but surely they are identifying all the sensory stressors in their lives, such as shopping, cooking, going out to movies and/or dinner, chores, touching and cuddling, organization and tidiness and, yes, sex. They are now identifying and understanding the stressors from both sides before considering the appropriate strategies to manage them.

An important consideration in relationship dynamics is that prevention is better than cure. Sometimes the emotional break-down in a troubled relationship has just gone too far for the relationship to be healed. So get in sync with your partner's sensory needs as soon as possible if you are not there yet!

Environmental goodness of fit

Although we have explored goodness of fit in relationships, I believe the process would be quite incomplete if we omitted the environment. Considering goodness of fit between people can be life changing, but we are still dependent on the other person for reciprocity in insight, awareness and action.

When considering goodness of fit between us and our environment, how-ever, we can usually remove most stressors, find our niches, create safe and happy work and living conditions and live life to the fullest.

WHAT IS GOODNESS OF FIT?

Goodness of fit in this context refers to how people and the environment relate to one another to produce a positive or negative outcome.

I am sure by now you know that the senses are stimulated through sensory input from our *environment*. Considering this major environmental effect can be the key to unlocking your potential and passion. I believe and have seen in my practice that when there is an optimum fit between individuals and their environment based on their sensory needs, they thrive, enjoy life and are productive. Therefore, we always aim for an environmental match or positive goodness of fit when we explore this phenomenon.

An entire industry has evolved around 'environmental psychology' proving that the environments in which we live, work and operate have a direct impact on our wellness and performance. Your environment is a multi-dimensional construct that refers to the physical, social and cultural aspects in your life. You must consider that all these elements will impact on the environment in which you operate. For our purposes I want to focus on the environment through sensory eyes. Although there are many other aspects impacting on the environment, I want to simplify this process by looking at it purely on a sensory level. You must ask yourself, how your environment is shaped by visual, auditory, tactile, smell, taste and movement input. Then implement a three-step strategy:

- **Step 1**: Revisit Chapter 1 and identify the sensory elements in your environment. Consider your home, work, social and cultural environ-ments. Where you live, who lives with you, where you work, how you get there, who you socialize with, what cultural activities you are involved in, etc.
- **Step 2**: Consider your sensory profile and resultant sensory needs as established by means of the checklists in Chapter 2.
- **Step 3**: Obtain goodness of fit with your environment. Satisfy your sensory needs within your environment as much as possible to obtain a positive goodness of fit. With an environment matching your sensory needs, you will be more passionate about what you do, experience more enjoyment and peace and achieve a good balance in your life.

Use this diagram to put your strategy into action:

Profile	Environment (sensory generated)	Goodness of fit
Sensation seekers (High thresholds, active interaction) Leaves	Unpredictability; variety; novelty; multi-sensory; crowds; people; large groups; activities; intense and frequent sensory input; surprise elements; open-plan offices; public transport; etc.	Yes
Sensation seekers (High thresholds, active interaction) Leaves	Predictability; structure; sameness; rigidity; quiet and contained spaces; routines; small groups or individual contact; gentle and diminished sensory input; closed office spaces; etc.	No
Sensation avoiders (Low thresholds, passive interaction) Deep roots	Predictability; structure; sameness; rigidity; quiet and contained spaces; routines; small groups or individual contact; gentle and diminished sensory input; closed office spaces; etc.	Yes
Sensation avoiders (Low thresholds, active interaction) Deep roots	Unpredictability; variety; novelty; multi-sensory; crowds; people; large groups; activities; intense and frequent sensory input; surprise elements; open-plan offices; public transport; etc.	No
Low registrators (High thresholds, active interactions) Branches	Intensifying sensory input – louder, brighter, harder, tighter; multi-sensory input; intense and frequent sensory input; open-plan offices; public transport; etc.	Yes
Low registrators (High thresholds, passive interactions) Branches	Decreased sensory input – softer, calmer, gentler, multi-sensory input; predictable and structured sensory input; quiet and calming spaces and situations; small groups of people; etc.	No
Sensory sensitives (Low thresholds, passive interactions) Roots	Decreased sensory input – softer, calmer, gentler, multi-sensory input; predictable and structured sensory input; quiet and calming spaces and situations; small groups of people; etc.	Yes
Sensory sensitives (Low thresholds, passive interactions) Roots	Intensifying sensory input – louder, brighter, harder, tighter; multi-sensory input; intense and frequent sensory input; open-plan offices; public transport	No

For those of you with typical thresholds, I have not allowed major goodness of fit categories for you. The reason is that your system neither over- nor under-responds to the sensory information coming from your environment. You can, however, use your sensory systems checklist to determine your low threshold systems (root systems, reduce or avoid) versus your high threshold systems (leaf systems, add).

Now let's be more practical and specific regarding environments. I want to illustrate the best goodness of fit options for sensory profiles in their environments. The strategies below have been derived from my current context and based on my clinical experience. I will be overindulgent purely because I want to make a point. Your situation, environment, socio-economic status, culture, age and beliefs might be different. In general I will be applying the rule that *less is more* for roots and *more is more* for leaves. Try to fit your current life into this context. Another important factor: humans are adaptable; you will find that you can cope with various different activities, situations, etc. not necessarily fitting your particular sensory profile. However, your profile is an indication of your comfort zone, in other words where and how you cope best and what will be optimal conditions for your productivity, peace and wellness.

Profile	Optimum sensory generated environments	
	Homes	Holidays
High threshold Leaves	Colourful; open-plan; entertainment orientated; within a city; apartment; busy section of a city or town	Overseas trips; busy tourist attractions; camping; adventure trips to the Amazon, North pole, Alaska, etc.; beach house in busy sea side town; large group excursions; etc.
Low threshold Roots	Neat; uncluttered; spacious; special room or area for quiet time; in a quiet section of a city or town; free standing home; good sound and temperature regulation; garden important to provide secluded spaces; close to work to minimize travelling;	Secluded areas; when on an overseas trip – one country; camping – must be organized, planned and scheduled, preferably in quiet, secluded area; beach house in small, secluded area; island vacations; cabin in mountains; private beaches; small group excursions; etc.

The two main profile categories were used to demonstrate the environment-person link more practically. It is also important to consider sensory systems to fine-tune the above suggestions. For example, considering the noise levels of the areas is important when you are dealing with a profile which includes an auditory sensitivity.

Summary

Whatever your sensory profile, your lifestyle, demands, culture, socio-economic status, dependency status and life roles, sensory overload is real and relevant. Each individual responds differently to life based on his or her inborn, primitive, genetic response to the environment via the senses. By acknowledging this hugely important fact and gaining as much insight into and understanding of this principle, and by acknowledging the positive traits of each profile, we can add love and value to and make any relationship blossom and grow. We can also create the best sensory in-sync environments for ourselves.

To Milandi de Villiers, Heloise Avenant, Lizanne du Plessis, Kulsum Bagus and Lyn Ziervolgel. Thank you for reading, and reading and more reading and your constructive feedback.

To my friends Cecile van Heerden and Chrisna Smit, I need another book to tell you how much you mean to me.

CHAPTER 5

Levels of sensory processing – sensory overload, stress and shutdown

Sensory information reaches individual brains at different and unique levels. There is a general truth that the brain somehow manages a fine equilibrium between focusing and attending to the important stuff, while ignoring the unimportant stuff. This balance is crucial for us to stay focused and attentive to complete a task, have a conversation or do whatever we may be busy doing. But even though this is the general truth, individuals register and respond to sensory input at different levels, intensities and frequencies.

While you are reading this, your brain does not identify the feeling of your sock inside your shoe. Your brain would have decided that it is not important information and would not recruit more brain messages to take the information to a conscious level. But if you are buying new running socks and trying them on in the shop, the situation will be different. Then the brain will respond to the information since it is necessary and important to help you decide whether you are buying the right socks.

I once started off a workshop by asking the question: "Who of you are feeling your sock inside your shoe?" One workshop delegate who actually did feel her socks at all times was amazed at the fact that no one else was experiencing the same feeling. This is a perfect example of different thresholds; people with low thresholds (roots of the tree) for the touch system can and often do feel their clothes, labels, socks, etc. almost always. It demands more work, effort and energy from the brain to process this unnecessary and unimportant information. Low threshold people will therefore often feel overloaded, stressed and tired faster. Their brains typically work harder and more frequently because they are attending to what high threshold people's brains would block out as unnecessary information. Owing to low threshold people's hyper-sensitivity to what is going on around them, they are typically more intuitive to their environments, people and world.

Life is, fast paced and demanding and multi-tasking is essential in order to cope. We often find ourselves in busy and stressful situations and recharging our batteries is something we need to diarize, it just doesn't come naturally. We typically operate in a world full of sensory input; we hear, see, taste, smell, move, touch and act. Sensory overload – the accumulation of sensory input – is therefore evident and prevalent in most people's lives. Sensory overload, a general state of 'too much for the brain', can and does often result in discomfort, irritation and stress. Sensory overload is a reality in life. Individuals with different sensory profiles reach sensory overload at different levels, intensities and frequencies. They experience and manage this differently.

The brain journey in level of responses

In order for us to understand the sensory intelligence process with regards to the unique and individual way in which we process information and how we cope with sensory overload, it is important to take a brief look at current research and theories on the brain. Understanding and insight are the key components to sensory intelligence. I have always found that clients implement sensory strategies far more successfully when they understand the underlying neuroscientific basis. Knowing why and when we need to implement certain strategies and understanding how our bodies and brains work with them, make them far more successful. With this in mind let's take a brief look at the following:

- Arousal theories – alert states of the brain
- The autonomic nervous system – the survival brain.

AROUSAL THEORIES

The arousal theories are very old and literature on the importance of arousal goes back as far as the 1940s. *Arousal* refers to the alert and conscious level of the brain that is necessary for us to stay awake and focused during the course of the day. We know that all sensory pathways and information have direct and indirect links with the brain stem – the seat of the reticular activating system. This is the main brain area facilitating optimum arousal – feeling and acting awake and alert. An important distinction between the senses is that the messages of pain, light touch, head movement and sound have a first-line, direct influence on the arousal centre of the brain. Therefore, input from these senses would potentially be more inclined to increase our arousal and overload us. Touch pressure, proprioception, smell and visual messages connect with the arousal centre more indirectly and do not have the same immediate overload potential.

The effect of the senses on arousal is a crucial part of sensory intelligence. When we use the senses we can either increase or decrease our arousal. In other words, we can use the senses to calm us down or to wake us up. This is discussed more in detail in Chapter 6.

We also need to look at the necessity of optimal arousal in order to obtain optimal performance. We know that we should be optimally alert and awake to focus and concentrate for optimum learning and working. The following diagram explains this well:

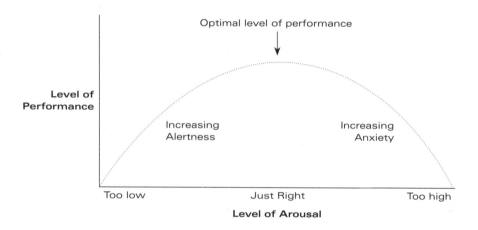

The two axes in the equation are the level of performance and the level of arousal. When arousal is optimal, we will have an optimal level of performance. Only when we are fully awake and alert are we functioning 100%, being focused and productive.

With arousal low, we are usually asleep or totally 'not there'. Then an increase in alertness will occur. Performance levels will start to increase and when the balance is right (in the middle), we will achieve optimal performance. This is the best point to be, your brain is optimally alert and awake and you can work or function at your best. When arousal increases too much, we get hyped up, anxious, flustered and our performance level will drop.

We need optimal arousal for optimum performance. Normal arousal is the optimum state in which we should try to stay throughout most of our day spent at work or during important activities. It is the 'just right' state of the brain to focus, pay attention and get the job done.

Normal/just right arousal is optimum and needed for work and daily living.

High arousal is characterized by a heightened, hyper-response with the brain going into over-drive. It is often associated with hyperactivity, agitation and anxiety. When we stay in high arousal for too long, our systems will eventually crash and go into shutdown.

A high arousal state is appropriate when we are at a sporting match supporting our home team or attending a rock concert, but contra-indicated for work.

Low arousal is indicated by a 'stand-by state', sometimes fatigue and lethargy, a quiet, non-responsive state and reduced focus and attention. Low arousal is necessary to start turning down our systems so that we can sleep at night – a state of decreased arousal – and sleep is vital for us to recharge our brains and systems to cope with the demands of living. Research links lack of sleep to increased stress, illness and certainly diminished performance.

Low arousal is not only necessary for sleep. We sometimes need to tap into this state during the course of a normal day. It is the ideal state to go into when you take a relaxing lunch break or just try to relax a little during the day.

A low arousal state is necessary for sleep but contra-indicated for work.

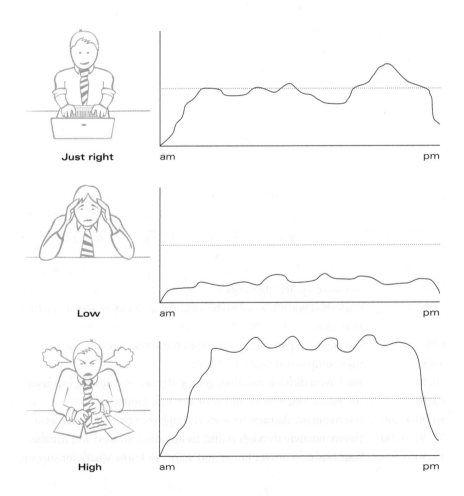

Just right   am   pm

Low   am   pm

High   am   pm

Our aim is always optimal arousal during the course of a day. Depending on the sensory events within your day (for example phone constantly ringing, boss yelling, difficult meeting, demanding children, etc.) your arousal level will be inclined to increase to reach high arousal. Then the use of self-regulation strategies (to calm or destress) is important. The next diagram depicts the course of a normal day with regard to arousal levels:

- We start the day in low arousal, as we wake up.
- As our day progresses our arousal levels are determined by the sensory events within our environment, work, home and expectations.
- When there is too much, too often, our arousal increases and goes into sensory overload.
- It is never a flat line, but rather an up and down curve of our systems and bodies coping with the demands of our lives.

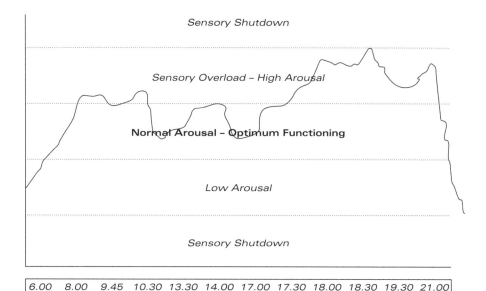

| 6.00 | 8.00 | 9.45 | 10.30 | 13.30 | 14.00 | 17.00 | 17.30 | 18.00 | 18.30 | 19.30 | 21.00 |

6.00	You wake up, feeling sleepy
7.00	You've had your first or maybe second cup of coffee and are getting more alert
8.00	You are driving in traffic, getting to the office, arousal increasing
9.45	Slight drop – you take a tea break
10.30	You have a difficult meeting, getting stressed and arousal increases
13.30	You take a lunch break and your alertness drop a little
14.00-17.00	You maintain alertness to work through the rest of the afternoon
17.30-18.00	You manoeuvre through traffic, feeling tired, stressed and irritable
18.30	Your husband arrives home and wants to know what's for supper.

	You need to bath and feed the children and check their homework. You feel very stressed and tired, and that the day should really get to an end. An accumulation of sensory input is evident here.
20.00	You heave a sigh of relief when the children fall asleep. You can sit down quietly, read the paper or watch your favourite TV program
21.00	You get a disturbing phone call from a family member. You feel anxious and stressed again and your arousal level increases again
After 21.00	You prepare for bed, have a nice warm bath with aromatherapy oils, burn a candle, listen to quiet music, your arousal levels drop and prepare you to go to bed, switch off the light and turn the brain off into 'park' or/shutdown.

The above is purely used as an example of a typical day in the life of a working mother. It will obviously differ from person to person but the principle stays the same: our level of arousal at any point in time is dependent on the activities, sensory events and stressors we experience daily.

AUTONOMIC NERVOUS SYSTEM

The autonomic nervous system is the primitive self-protection system of the brain. It warns us of present danger and helps the body prepare to go into a fight/flight/fright mode. Depending on the situation and personal threshold system, we respond protectively towards input in different manners of fight/flight or fright. Fight is going into an active resistant mode, applying force to counteract the danger and protect yourself. Flight is fleeing, getting away as fast and as soon as possible. Fright is fear, the body going into protective mode upon realising danger. These reactions are often masked by other behaviours and we don't always identify them as autonomic nervous system responses. Specific manifestations of some of these important responses are:

Flight	Fright (Fear)	Fight
Distractibility	Whining, crying, clinging	Frustration
Redirecting	Fearfulness	Outbursts
Escape behaviour	Reluctance to try new	Aggression
Boredom	things, activities or places	Resistance
Removing yourself from a	Withdrawal, hiding	Acting out
particular situation	Saying: "I can't"	Saying: "I won't, NO"

The body also shows physical signs when the autonomic nervous system has been triggered: an increase in heart rate, sweating, nausea, pallor, fast, shallow breathing, diluted pupils and the hairs on your skin raising are all signs that the body is under immediate stress.

These responses are very real and important for all of us, especially for self-protection and self-preservation. These responses are more intense, frequent and prevalent in people with low thresholds. The sensory defensive group (the most severe category of sensory sensitivity), the real deep roots, experience autonomic nervous system responses more intensely, frequently and prominently. Because their brains often experience the world more intensely, their autonomic nervous system just kicks in more intensely and frequently in an attempt at self-protection. What is often a normal, day-to-day occurrence, can be perceived as potentially dangerous by the sensory defensive group and result in an autonomic nervous system self protective action. For instance, standing in line and being touched accidentally by a stranger from behind can trigger a protective response. This is a typical but unconscious reaction from a root person, often misunderstood and perceived negatively by the bystander. This is real and occurs regularly in the life of a sensory defensive root person.

Sensory overload

Sensory overload results from an accumulation of sensory information in individuals throughout the course of their normal day. We know that in certain situations and at certain times of the day we are more inclined to experience sensory overload. One situation can also lead to sensory overload for one person but not for another. For instance a noisy birthday party can create sensory overload for someone who is auditory sensitive but not for someone who is auditory seeking, or has a normal threshold for auditory input. Getting into a full lift can cause sensory overload in someone who is tactile sensitive but not necessarily for others with higher tactile thresholds.

During sensory overload arousal levels often increase and fight/flight/fight reactions can be triggered. Generally when we are sick or stressed, we reach sensory overload much faster and more frequently, and experience it more intensely. We also tend to cope better with sensory input in the morning rather than later in the day. This is generally true for most people. After a good night's sleep we all seem to process sensory information more easily. The brain has had a chance to rest to a degree and is fresh and ready to tackle a new day. Sensory inputs also have an accumulative effect; as the day progresses we need to process more information and the brain gets more tired while reaching overload faster later in the day. The name of the so-called suicide hour between 5 and 7 pm makes a lot of sense, especially in a home where there are children. This is the time when the children need to be fed and bathed, their homework checked, supper prepared, etc. There are just to many sensory demands after a full day of sensory input accumulation with both the children's and the parent's sensory systems on the verge of depletion. It's often a recipe for a disaster.

The bottom line is, sensory overload is a real hurdle in daily life.

I have compiled a list of possible sensory overload occurrences that we experience in the home and work environment and also suggested activities of self-care:

Parenting issues

Parenting children today is no easy feat. To add to this demanding task, our family times are eroded by tight work schedules, TV, commuting time, school and community projects, etc. The following events and routines are know to create sensory overload and have the potential to cause explosive situations:

- Suicide hour; 5-7 at night, especially with children 6 and younger
- Birthday parties
- Getting children to bed at night
- Getting children dressed
- Meal times
- Bath time
- Social interactions with peers; aggressive behaviours, refusal to socialize, etc.
- Sibling rivalry.

Relationship issues

After reading Chapter 4 you have probably seen yourself and your spouse or partner in a new light. Choices and participation in the following can potentially create sensory overload in the root and misunderstanding in the leaf. Couples may disagree on the following as they unknowingly face the reality of thresholds determining our choices, likes and dislikes:

- Holidays and weekends away
- Going out for dinner, movies, etc.
- Chores in and around the house
- Cuddling and touching
- Sex
- Feeling loved and appreciated
- Clutter versus tidiness, creating order
- In-laws
- Managing conflict
- Discipline of children
- Doing things together
- Shopping.

Work issues

Work is a hard reality as all of us need to earn a living. In this process we are thrown into situations, environments and expectations. You need to meet deadlines, produce quality work, giving of your time, skill and effort. These are the typical culprits in most work environments that have the potential to create sensory overload:

- Traffic
- Meetings
- Noise
- Colleagues
- Boss
- Tasks and expectations
- Seating and position in the office
- Electronics: phones, air conditioners, faxes, computers, etc.
- Work hours
- Targets and deadlines
- Engaging with and entertaining clients
- Change
- Working from home.

Sensory overload is real and prevalent. How do we get there? What happens then? Where does stress come in?

Levels of sensory processing

Levels of sensory processing refer to the stages that the brain and body go through based on the daily sensory demands of our lives. These levels are a normally generated response for all individuals. If you consider the different stages you will note that all of us go through them from time to time. The key here is frequency and intensity. When you frequently spend a lot of time in stages 3 to 5 it is likely that you will suffer from too much stress and ultimately burn out. These stages are therefore crucial to consider when managing your sensory input in life and could be seen as a stress management strategy.

The levels through which we process sensory information can be described in the following order (our arousal and associated anxiety and stress levels increase through each level):

Level 1 – I'm OK
This is a level of comfort enabling us to cope with all information from the environment in a productive and optimal manner. When at this level, we can

work productively, deal with our life demands, care for our families and fulfil our societal roles.

Level 2 – I'm stressed

Level two refers to a state where drive and output are accelerated by workload, intensity and expectation, the so called 'good stress'. Stress is a positive element keeping us going and in constant motion. It provides the motivation and drive to continue and proceed with what is important. We all sometimes need a bit of a kick in the butt to get going, and here added pressure and demands can help us to get through our daily demands.

Level 3 – I'm in overload

This is a level where work-load intensity and expectation start to reach a stage beyond the physical capacity of an individual resulting in more negative stress, discomfort and a drop in performance levels. Individuals will become irritable, tetchy, short tempered and tend to over-react owing to the build up of sensory overload. Overload happens when there are more demands made on us, more intensely and more frequently for us to cope with. This is often a result of too much seeing, hearing, smelling, touching, moving and tasting for our brain. This is the stage where we say: "Stop the world, I want to get off!" Overload therefore refers to too much sensory input and is a clear warning sign to reduce expectation and input/output.

Level 4 – I'm out of control

At the out of control level the individual starts to experience significant break-down of function. This level is marked with negative emotions such as fear, fright, aggression, hostility, antagonism and things get blown out of proportion. Owing to the negative emotional reaction, this level is marked with conflict at home, at work or in a social environment. This is a negative phase for everyone involved as it breaks down relationships, teamwork, personal effectiveness and cohesion.

Level 5 – Shutdown

A shutdown phase is where our systems literally 'go on strike' and we become depersonalized and dissociated from the environment and situation. There usually is a break down of individual abilities. At this level physical removal from the environment is necessary. People often get sick at this stage. It is a classic sign of burn-out. It is totally counter-productive and impacts negatively on our health and wellness.

IDEAL LEVELS

It is important to aim at staying between levels 1 and 2 of sensory processing. Moving into level 3 becomes the warning signal for us that we should reduce our workload or, more importantly, self-regulate – *TAKE FIVE, TAKE A BREAK* (see Chapter 6). Levels 4 and 5 are negative, unproductive and very difficult to get out of. It is much harder to move from level 5 back to level 1 rather than just moving between the first 2 levels. This is an obvious basis for stress management. Stress management in my opinion is often more valuable when considered from this primitive, sensory perspective. First, consider your thresholds and responses, then find your best-fit option for sensory self-regulation. When the goodness of fit between your thresholds, sensory responses, sensory needs and life expectations are ideal, you will find it easy to stay within the first two levels. It is when there is a bad goodness of fit that you get stuck between levels 3 to 5 and suffer as a result. This diagram (The arousal wheel) explains the states more clearly:

THE AROUSAL WHEEL: INCREASING AROUSAL

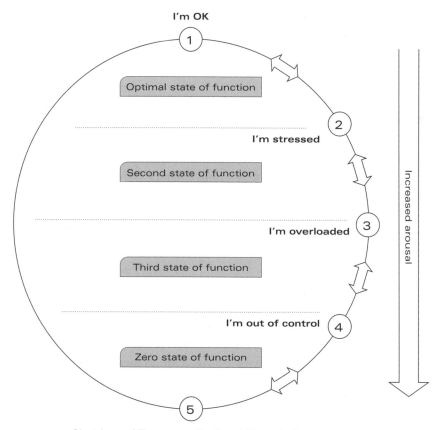

I'm OK

1

Optimal state of function

2

I'm stressed

Second state of function

Increased arousal

I'm overloaded   3

Third state of function

I'm out of control   4

Zero state of function

5

Shutdown / Depersonalization / Dissociation

DECREASING AROUSAL

We also need to consider arousal levels dropping. Arousal levels start to drop when we go to bed at night. We are okay, then start to feel tired towards the end of the day, we start to feel sleepy and when we fall asleep we become 'unconscious' and our systems move into shutdown. Usually and hopefully this state remains for 6-8 hours so that our systems can rest and recharge.

The levels through which we go to unwind and prepare for sleep at the end of the day can be described as follows (our arousal decreases through each level):

Level 1 – I'm OK

This is a level of comfort enabling us to cope with all information from the environment in a productive and optimal manner. At this level, we can work productively, deal with our life demands, care for our family and fulfil our societal roles.

Level 2 – I'm tired

Level two refers to a state where the body is starting to unwind, turning down the engine and feeling the fatigue and demands of the day create a sense of physical and emotional exhaustion.

Level 3 – I'm sleepy

The body relaxes and the brain's arousal levels decrease; we are feeling less awake, more sleepy and drowsy. Our brain functions are diminishing and our attention and focus reduced.

Level 4 – I'm 'unconscious'

Arousal has decreased further; our brain has found a parking space and is tuning out. We are in a light sleep state and all systems are turning down volume, closing down and preparing for a sleep state necessary to recharge the body.

Level 5 – Shutdown

A shutdown phase is where our systems literally shut down and tune out. We go into a deep sleep and register nothing on a conscious level. This process is crucial and we go through it at night to prepare us for sleep. At an unconscious level the brain remains working to keep your body alive.

The next diagram explains the zones and states of arousal for both increasing arousal (more anxiety) and decreasing arousal (sleepiness).

- The optimal zone of functioning lies between 1 and 2 and is ideal for daily work.
- The second zone of functioning lies between 2 and 3 and is characterized by an increase in stress (high arousal) or fatigue (low arousal).

In high arousal this zone can be considered the so-called 'good stress' which is the driving force and facilitator to extend us. We are productive in this zone and feel the need to up the levels due to demands.

- The third zone of functioning lies between 3 and 4 and is characterized by sensory overload (high arousal) or sleepiness (low arousal). Remember that we can also feel so tired during the course of a day that we become sleepy. This is an unproductive zone where we cannot fulfil our daily roles of work and taking care of our family.
- The zone of zero functioning lies between 4 and 5 and is characterized by out-of-control behaviours and shutting down. Although this zone is applicable and necessary at night for sleep you should not find yourself there during the course of a normal work day. There are, however, a large percentage of people who go into shutdown during the course of a normal day as a protective response to sensory overload and the accumulation of input. Classic burn-out can also be associated with this zone of functioning.

COMBINED AROUSAL WHEEL

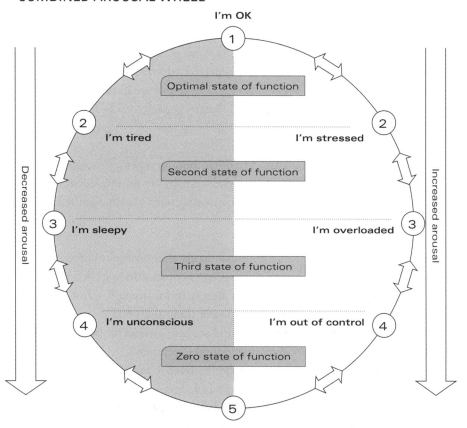

The practical use of the arousal theory will be evident in Chapter 6 when we look at using sensory strategies for self-regulation.

Sensory processing by different profiles

Our sensory processing responses, namely sensation avoiding or sensation seeking, differ from person to person. We are all somewhere on the continuum between sensory defensiveness (roots) at one end and sensory seekers (leaves) at the other end. It would be most appropriate to talk about manifesting sensory defensive patterns to a mild, moderate or severe degree. The same applies to sensory seeking behaviours: we might be seeking sensory input to a mild, moderate or severe degree.

Mild sensory defensive or seeking behaviours are probably very common and most of us are in this area of the continuum. Moderate sensory defensive or seeking behaviours happen when these processing patterns start to increase in frequency and intensity and cause irritation and difficulty for people with these profiles. They become severe defensive behaviours (real deep roots) and severe seeking behaviours (highest leaves) when the frequency and intensity of behaviours not only cause irritation quickly, but also start to impact negatively on how we operate at work, in our homes and in our lives in general.

Severe defensiveness can be observed in about 20% of the population, considering paediatric and other appropriate research. For this group, individual treatment plans for self-care is vital and effective to reduce occurrences of overload and shutdown. We discuss intervention plans in detail in Chapter 7.

The continuum of profiles can be graphically presented as follows:

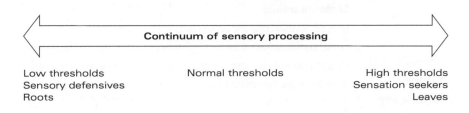

In practice I have found that root (low threshold) people reach sensory overload faster, but then tend to hover in this state for a while before reaching shutdown. They are, however, more intuitive about their body states and seem to be more aware when sensory overload is becoming evident, and they quickly identify that their bodies are 'feeling out of sync'. They tend to suffer faster and more intensely from sensory overload, which leads to stress.

Most of my root clients express the need for breaks, owing to sensory overload, and make an effort to build this into their normal day.

Leaf (high threshold) people in contrast take a long time to reach sensory overload. Their state of sensory overload is short. Remember that their brain can tolerate more sensory input for longer periods of time owing to the continuous and extensive habituation process. When high threshold people do reach sensory overload they tend to flip into shutdown much quicker because their brains and systems are already so overloaded when they first realize it. They do seem to be less aware of their states and must be coached towards recognizing the importance of stress management more specifically. They often realize too late when their bodies are in overload and then often need an extended period to de-stress.

Remember the aim is always to self-regulate in order to reduce sensory overload and prevent shutdown at all costs.

The following diagram illustrates quadrant profile distributions (in other words, your sensory profile tendency) on the sensory profile together with the build up towards sensory overload and shutdown:

SENSORY PROCESSING LEVELS

Threshold	What happens	What to do
	Low registration Under-responding to environmental info, miss environmental cues, unaware of many sounds, sights, smells, tastes, movement, may appear aloof and/or withdrawn ↓	Knowledge and insight, lifestyle choices, career planning
High neurological thresholds (High tolerance)	**Sensation seeking** Seek out novel, intense and added environmental stimuli, active, on the go, continuously engaging, fidgety, excitable, energetic, poor organization and concentration ↓	Creating opportunities for novel, intense and increased sensory interaction
	Sensory overload Excessive and constant environmental input, distractibility, over-arousal, overload, reduced productivity, not meeting deadlines or finishing work, stress ↓	Self-regulate
	Sensory shutdown Shutdown/Depersonalization/Dissociation	Crisis management

Threshold	What happens	What to do
	Sensory sensitive Not adequate filtering and ignoring of environmental input, constant awareness, orienting, reaction and responding to noise activity, smells, taste, movement, sights	Knowledge and insight, lifestyle choices, career planning Mental rehearsal and Preparation
	↓ **Sensation avoiding** Avoiding certain situations and activities that might be potential for sensory overload, impact on social interaction, fear of the unknown and unexpected, not always willing or comfortable with exposure to new situations and activities	Avoid or anticipate, mental rehearsal and preparation
Low neurological thresholds (Low tolerance)	↓ **Sensory overload** Constant sensations from the environment, poor filtering of information, over-responding to excess information, distractibility, irritability, fight-fright-flight, over-arousal, overload, reduced productivity, not meeting deadlines or finishing work, stress	Self-regulate
	↓ **Sensory shutdown** Shutdown/Depersonalization/Dissociation	Crisis management

Then, what do we do for each band to obtain optimal functioning and productivity? Inside each state the major intervention component is illustrated.

Coping with sensory overload

This can be a complicated process when considering what is happening in each brain with sensory overload, since we cannot really go and fine-tune our brains to process information differently. I believe a general intervention approach considering all aspects is important and I discuss this extensively in Chapter 7. Gaining knowledge and insight regarding our bodies' responses to the environment is the crucial first step. My general rule for coping with sensory overload is the following:

1 Avoid/Add

2 Anticipate

3 Self-regulate

If you are a root – avoid sensory input.
If you are a leaf – add sensory input.
If you cannot do either – anticipate.
Prepare yourself for what is going to happen.
And finally, self-regulate – using the senses to control overload and arousal.

Since self-regulation is so critical, the next chapter is dedicated in full to this important intervention strategy.

"TAKE FIVE, TAKE A BREAK": self-regulate – stress management with a difference

A few weeks ago I was driving on the highway in Cape Town. Passing me on the fast lane was a black BMW X5 – a really fancy car, the driver a middle-aged male dressed in a smart business suit, obviously rich and powerful. What caught my attention is that he wasn't talking on his cellphone without his hands-free kit, that sucking on a pink dummy! I curiously searched for the baby seat in the back of the car, but to my amazement there was no car seat. We eventually stopped at the same chemist just off the highway. He got out of his car, removed the dummy from his mouth and put it in his pocket. I know this sounds bizarre, but it is true. Although seemingly inappropriate and immature, he was using the oldest and most primitive form of self-regulation. The sucking action is the first reflexive process a baby goes through in order to self-calm and thereby self-regulate. It is through the sucking process that the baby feels calmed and nurtured. It is appropriate and relevant for babies, but we are eventually weaned off our dummies. Sucking on a cigarette, eating and chewing to manage our stress are some of the self-regulatory strategies that replace this primitive action (sucking) of calming the brain and the body.

So let me take you through the theory and application of self-regulation (no dummies allowed).

To Wilsia Metz and everyone at Metz Press,
When you couldn't get me writing, you got me running!
Thank you for seeing the potential of this book and making it happen.

CHAPTER 6

TAKE FIVE, TAKE A BREAK, self-regulate – stress management with a difference

A few weeks ago I was driving on the highway in Cape Town. Passing me on the side was a black BMW X5, a really fancy car, the driver a middle-aged male, dressed in a smart business suit, obviously rich and powerful. What caught my attention is that he wasn't talking on his cellphone without his hands-free kit, but sucking on a pink dummy! I curiously searched for the baby seat in the back of the car, but to my amazement there was no car seat. We eventually stopped at the same chemist just off the highway. He got out of his car, removed the dummy from his mouth and put it in his pocket. I know this sounds bizarre, but it is true. Although seemingly inappropriate and im-mature, he was using the oldest and most primitive form of self-regulation. The sucking action is the first reflexive process a baby goes through in order to self-calm and thereby self-regulate. It is through the sucking process that the baby feels calmed and nurtured. It is appropriate and relevant for babies, but we are eventually weaned off our dummies. Sucking on a cigarette, eating and chewing to manage our stress are some of the self-regulatory strategies that replace this primitive action (sucking) of calming the brain and the body.

So let me take you through the theory and application of self-regulation (no dummies allowed!).

Daily modulation of the senses

We go through a daily process of changing arousal levels, which affect our attention. Our work and living situations contribute to emotions, behaviour and how we interact socially. We are on the move at all times, producing work and/or learning and/or studying and/or caring for our families. Our process of sensory modulation is never a flat line process but rather an ebb and flow of high and low peaks. Our systems fluctuate according to our life roles, demands, health status and sensory load. This can be visually presented as follows:

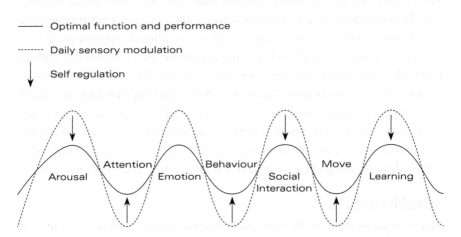

We have an optimal level of functioning as represented by the solid-line curve. Then, depending on our thresholds, demands and expectations, our sensory modulation curves, represented by the broken-line curve, fluctuate between peaks either too low or too high. It is like fine-tuning a radio to find the right station. Finding the right frequency is by a process of self-regulation and illustrated by the arrows. When we are too high (anxious, over-stressed, over-excited), we bring our systems down (we self-calm) and when we are too low (bored, lethargic, tired, sleepy), we bring our systems up (we self-alert). It is through this constant regulatory process that we keep the brain and body in equilibrium.

The key here is that sensory input continuously passes the reticular activating system en route to the cortex. The reticular activating system (among other brain structures) is responsible for us feeling awake, alert or asleep. Therefore, it is through this crucial brain process that we can self-regulate through the senses – the underpinning of effective stress management.

The process of self-regulation

What is self-regulation and why is it necessary? We can say that self-regulation is the process by which we change our levels of arousal and alertness to be appropriate for the task at hand. It is often an unconscious process. Have you ever observed people in church during the sermon or at a conference or meeting where they have to stay focused and attentive, while sitting still? If you watch carefully you will notice some of the following behaviours: doodling with their pens on the paper, twirling their hair, biting their pens, scratching their faces (and sometimes picking their noses), tapping their feet, etc. These are all methods that the body unconsciously uses to stay focused and alert, but are often referred to as habits. Have you ever wondered why we are offered peppermints at conferences? Because the smell and taste of peppermint alerts the brain. Combine that with a chewing or sucking action and the brain kicks into a full alert state, optimal for concentration and focus. A German company building large trucks is investigating the possibility of using vibrating seatbelts and releasing a minty smell in the cabin – all efforts to maintain an optimal state of arousal for the truck drivers who have to stay awake and alert for hours on end. They will be able to drive for longer in a more alert and awake state, reducing safety risks.

SENSORY HABITS

When we consider how the brain processes information and reacts to sensory input, it makes us think about habits in a different way. The brain has an automatic drive to reach balance or homeostasis. In other words, trying to self-regulate or calm or alert the system could potentially be an automatic response of the brain to achieve balance. If you are in the habit of doodling on a piece of paper while talking on the phone, this could merely be your brain's way of ensuring that you stay alert and focused. On this basis we can assume that similar habits are employed to meet a sensory need.

When we investigate why, how and when habits occur, this becomes the first step towards knowing what to do in situations that require self-regulation. For example, if you have a tendency to rub your fingers, (I know, it is a strange habit, but most of them are), asking why and when you do this, you may discover that it is when you feel anxious or stressed, or before an important event.

Looking at how you do it, may indicate that by rubbing your fingers you are using deep touch pressure, a sensory input that is known to calm the brain. Our sensory habits can therefore indicate whether we are stressed, tired, anxious or bored. Knowing what is happening between ourselves and the situation can help us manage these situations more effectively.

DEVELOPMENT FROM BABYHOOD

Self-regulation in babies is crucial to maintaining a state of arousal, where the baby can be awake at times to be stimulated, and change to self-calming in order to fall asleep. The sucking reflex prepares the baby for feeding but also has a generally calming effect. Sensory overload in babies can contribute to excessive crying and inability to settle.

As children mature and develop, they learn to access more brain structures to help them to stay focused, be calm and manage their worlds. It is important to remember that there is a connection between the frontal cortex (part of the CEO) and the emotional brain that is only fully mature in children by the age of 10. This explains the immature and inappropriate behaviours and emotions during the first 10 years of life. Our toddlers are not yet ready to rationalize and understand the world cognitively. This process of integrating all brain parts to self-regulate is gradual and unconscious, but an important processes that assists us to cope with life.

SELF-REGULATION FOR SCHOOL CHILDREN

Research indicates that children today have major problems with concentration in the classrooms owing to their passive state. Most children today are stuck behind computer and TV screens, not moving enough, no longer engaged in physical outdoors play, and to crown it all physical education in schools has been terminated. We are raising an overweight, unfit and passive generation. I know this sounds harsh, but unfortunately it is also true. Children need to move; it is through movement that their brains grow and develop and the movement system is one of the strongest systems to help with self-regulation. We should incorporate movement strategies in classrooms; movement works.

If you are stuck behind a computer, busy working and feel your concentration slipping, getting tired and losing focus, what do you instinctively do? You get up, don't you? Moving out of your chair is a natural response of the brain and the body to regain focus. And we wonder why children can't sit still in classrooms anymore. Their brains are crying out for help in the movement division! Get your children away from passive entertainment and get them moving – and move with them! The principle of self-regulation through the senses is a powerful process that is used by a handful of teachers in our schools. Given the current issues in education it should be used more widely.

The old command "sit still and pay attention" needs to change. Most children can either sit still or pay attention. They need to move to get sensory-motor input in order to focus and pay attention.

SELF-REGULATION FOR ADULTS

As adults we go through a daily ebb and flow process of sensory modulation as depicted in the diagram on page 132. When you feel you are getting anxious or hyped up, you may stop, take a deep breath, and get yourself a cup of coffee after which you may feel ready to carry on. You've used your senses to calm yourself – you have used your mouth to suck and the caffeine is an added stimulant which peps you up. You have also moved and breathed, both strong self-regulatory strategies.

When you feel tired or sleepy, you also get up, stretch, take a bathroom break and maybe drink a glass of cold water. You are again utilizing your movement, mouth (oral-motor) systems and temperature to make yourself feel more alert.

You realize on an unconscious level when your arousal is either too low (feeling flat, tired, lethargic) or too high (feeling hyped up, anxious) and you automatically try to regain equilibrium. You self-monitor your world and recognize the need to change or maintain your arousal states.

Bottom-up versus top-down inhibition

Inhibition refers to a process by which we basically control the amount of information that reaches our brains. It is a way to control the unique process of filtering within the brain. There is a natural tendency for the brain to obtain equilibrium and you will feel when you are spiralling out of control; you will experience the urge to act to regain your balance. Remember that your genetic thresholds play a crucial role here; roots go into sensory overload faster and feel out of control more frequently whereas leaves often realize too late that their systems are depleted.

There are two major ways of obtaining this crucial equilibrium, namely through top-down inhibition or through bottom-up inhibition.

Bottom-up inhibition

In this instance we utilize the lower, sensory parts of the brain to control the cortex. We use smell, taste, sight, hearing, touch and movement. Sensory messages from our body are sent to numerous brain structures and the cortex. As a result we become alert and organized. It is the sensory root of self-regulation and highly effective.

Top-down inhibition

In this instance we utilize the cortex, the higher brain structures, through mental preparation and/or self talk to regain control and organization. We basically control our lower brain structures and function with input from the cortex consciously thinking and reasoning about it. It is the cognitive root of self-regulation and also effective. However, I have found when in serious sensory overload this cognitive root seems to get stuck easily. Utilizing the senses then often seems to work better and more effectively, and the effect lasts longer.

Self-regulation and your sensory profile

A combination of bottom-up and top-down inhibition is recommended to self-regulate optimally. I do advocate the use of bottom-up inhibition more strongly since it contains the sensory elements.

Studying your Sensory Systems Checklist (Chapter 3) would assist you in choosing the best method of self-regulation. Those systems which showed a high threshold pattern would most likely be the best methods of self-regulation. In other words, those systems with a score of +2 to +10, should be your first choice as they would potentially be more suited to calm and organize your brain via the senses. I have explained various possibilities in Chapter 3; please refer back to this section.

Sensory properties

The senses can be used to calm or to alert which will organize the brain. Although individual sensory profiles differ, there is a general rule on which sensory input generally contributes to arousal states and how it is done. This is an important consideration when we use the bottom-up approach to self-regulate.

The following diagram gives examples of the sensory properties of each sensory system:

Sense	Calming/Inhibitory (used when in over-arousal)	Alerting/Excitory (used when in under-arousal)
Tactile	Deep touch (firm, hard pressure)	Light touch (tickle, gentle stroking)
Auditory	Soft, whisper, classical baroque music	Loud, intense, rock music
Visual	Soft, gentle colours and light	Bright light, colours, clutter
Vestibular	Slow, rhythmic movement	Fast, irregular movements
Proprioception	Heavy muscle work against resistance	Heavy muscle work against resistance
Taste	Warm, smooth, sweet	Cold, sour, spicy, minty, crunchy
Smell	Lavender, chamomile	Mint, citrus

Tactile properties (the skin receptors)
Deep, firm and hard touch is calming and often used for self-calming and regulation. It is for this reason that we swaddle babies; being in a tight cocoon of soft

blanket calms the baby. Deep massage uses exactly the same principle and is an excellent way to make the body feel good and controlled. On the other hand, if anyone tickles you (this is light touch), you would start to feel over-aroused and hyped up. Especially for individuals with low tactile thresholds, gentle, soft tickling strokes on the skin are extremely uncomfortable and they avoid this at all times. For many of the tactile defensive clients that I've worked with, it works well to get someone else to lie on top of their bodies. This gives them strong and hard touch and calms them down. Heavy blankets are also effective as they create warmth and are calming.

Auditory properties (the hearing receptors)

Listening to calming, soft music which has an even pitch and intensity often makes us feel calm and relaxed. Rock, fast paced and high-pitched music, on the other hand, increases the alertness of the brain. You would certainly feel hyped up, over-alert and excited when attending a Robbie Williams concert. You will probably be jumping up and down, screaming, yelling and shouting. I cannot imagine doing the same when attending a symphony concert at a theatre. The choice of music for calming is a personal thing and I would suggest using trial and error to find what works for you. Music has strong properties to either calm or alert the brain through the auditory system. We also need to consider other sounds, for instance the sound of water, the sea, birds, etc. which also tend to be very calming for most people.

Visual properties (the sight receptors)

Sharp and contrasting colours tend to increase alertness in the brain whereas soft, gentle colours do the opposite. A cluttered environment will also send more information through to the brain, alerting and arousing it. A neat and organized environment from a visual perspective is often noted to be extremely useful for people with low thresholds (roots). I am always interested to see how people decorate their homes; roots have a tendency to prefer the less is more approach with natural, blended colours. Leaves often experiment with bolder colours and would be more inclined to bring them into their decorating styles. Even the choice of the colour clothes that we wear can have a threshold origin. Lighting is another important consideration; we know that certain fluorescent lights can be very distracting and therefore over-arousing to the brain. Natural lighting is the preferred form to enhance performance.

Vestibular properties (the inner ear receptors)

Gentle, smooth, rocking and slow movements are calming for the brain. A mother with a small baby will instinctively start to rock a baby. Gentle rocking is, however, suggested and not the jumping and thumping we often see with mothers. Lying in a hammock on a deserted beach, gently swaying from side to side, is a picture of an idyllic scene many of us may be drooling over. It is this gentle, rhythmic movement in a hammock that will calm and relax you. On the other hand, getting on a roller-coaster ride is going to give you a thrill, excitement, wake up your brain and put you in a state of hyper arousal!

Proprioceptive properties (the body position receptors)

In sensory integration we call proprioception the universal modulator. We all know how alert and organized we feel following physical exercise. Whenever we increase the resistance of movement we load the proprioceptive pathway more intensely and as a result increase our sense of calm and organization. Resistance exercises (weight training, paddling or canoeing, etc.) in general seem to be more beneficial not only for a sense of calm, but also from a health perspective. When we are mad, angry and upset, hitting a boxing bag has calming effects and our anger will dissipate. Moving furniture and heavy garden digging are tiring, but extremely therapeutic.

Taste properties (the mouth and tongue receptors)

Eating and using food as a general self-calming strategy is as old as time itself. However, using it in an uncontrolled manner is also unhealthy and not recommended. It is through the combination of the taste receptors and the chewing action (proprioception) in the mouth that we obtain a sense of feeling good. I also believe that the mere act of smoking is using the oral structures to self-regulate. Add nicotine to the equation and you have a potent yet deadly form of self-regulation.

Which peppermints do you prefer, the ones you suck or the ones you chew? This preference indicates your unique and individual style of processing.

Think about anything that is warm and calming; we feel relaxed and calm when we sit outside in the sun. Having a hot drink before we go to bed is a way of decreasing our arousal, in other words to calm us down. Furthermore smooth and sweet tastes are also calming.

Cold temperatures are more alerting. When we have difficulty waking up in the morning, a coldish shower will certainly do the trick. We also feel more alert after we've had a cold drink, ice water or an ice-cream as opposed to having a warm cup of soup or hot chocolate. Sour and spicy tastes will alert the brain and crunchy textures also have an organizing effect.

Smell properties (the nose receptors)

There is an entire industry of aromatherapy using the sense of smell from a health and wellness perspective. Generally, we know that lavender and chamomile are calming fragrances whereas mint and citrus are alerting. I recommend the use of smell for individuals where it can be contained, for instance using aromatherapy oils in your bathtub or shower. But I would be reluctant to use them in groups or open spaces, purely based on the fact that thresholds differ. Some people might be very put off by certain smells that are not noxious or offensive to others. Remember that the sense of smell is quite powerful and triggers emotion and memory simultaneously.

TAKE FIVE, TAKE A BREAK

TAKE FIVE, TAKE A BREAK literally means take five (use the five primary self-regulation strategies discussed below) and also, take the time to rest and recharge. The take-five principles are based on the Alert Program developed by Shellenberger and Williams, two USA trained occupational therapists. The programme is in turn based on the brain concepts as discussed in Chapters 5 and 6, namely arousal states, inhibition, sensory properties, sensory processing and self-regulation. The process of attaining, maintaining or changing arousal states is often unconscious but based on an innate drive to seek and receive the sensory-motor input our brains and bodies need.

How does your engine run?
We use the concept of an engine when working with levels of arousal. Your body is like an engine, sometimes it runs on low, sometimes it runs on high, but when it runs just right, you are focused, attentive and productive. This simple, yet effective analogy can be extended and used when we look at ways to manipulate brain arousal levels for optimum functioning. This insight process has two stages:
  • Recognize your arousal states/engine levels (see page 125)
  • Recognize and use self-regulation strategies for your unique processing style.

Engine levels/arousal states
Your state of arousal can fluctuate between three:
  • Too high
  • Just right
  • Too low.

Take five – the five primary self-regulation strategies
So what are the primary self-regulation strategies?
  • Put something in your mouth
  • Move
  • Touch

- Look
- Listen.

As you read through the list of possible activities, choices or habits with regards to the five primary self-regulatory systems, make the connection of which ones you personally use, when and how you use them. It will give you some insight into your individual self-regulatory preferences. It might also put some quirky, odd behaviours and habits in a brand new, acceptable perspective! You will possibly be more likely to use these activities/actions when stressed, in deep concentration or when bored.

PUT SOMETHING IN YOUR MOUTH (ORAL-MOTOR INPUT)

When we put something in our mouths there is a synergy of the senses of taste, smell, touch and proprioception. Through this combination we change arousal levels. This form of self-regulation is often referred to as using 'brain food'.

- *What you do:* Blowing, sucking, swallowing, biting, crunching, chewing, licking
- *How it feels or tastes:* Physical feeling of resistance when biting, crunching, chewing, sucking and blowing; the tastes of sour, sweet, salty, spicy or bitter; the temperature of food such as hot chocolate, cold sucker, or warm soup
- *With what:* Whistle, straw, bubbles, musical instrument, exercise water bottle, sweets, biltong, rubber tubing, fruit, crackers, pretzels, bubble gum, bagels, popcorn, carrots, etc.

Inappropriate/unhealthy strategies

Overeating, compulsive eating, smoking, unhealthy food choices, sucking on dummies (for adults).

MOVE (VESTIBULAR AND PROPRIOCEPTIVE INPUTS)

When we move, the brain gets feedback from the vestibular organs in the inner ear, the body's GPS, as well as input from the proprioceptors located in the muscles and joints. Based on the changes in head position, intensity, frequency and resistance of movement, we stimulate the movement system in various ways.

- *Oscillation (up and down):* Horse riding, jumping, sitting and bouncing on a therapy ball, jumping on a trampoline, see-saw, riding a lift
  Sport: running
- *Linear (front and back/side to side):* Hammock, rocking in a rocking chair
  Sport: biking
- *Rotary (circular):* Turning on an office swivel chair, riding a rollercoaster
  Sport: gymnastics, ballet

- *Inverted (upside down):* Hanging upside down on barre or rings, somer-saults, head stands
  Sport: gymnastics
- *Proprioception:* Moving furniture, lifting firewood, pulling or pushing a cart, climbing stairs, hitting a boxing bag
  Sport: rugby, swimming, wrestling, kick boxing.

Inappropriate/unhealthy strategies
Unsafe movement choices. You should have a medical check-up prior to start-ing any exercise regime.

TOUCH (TACTILE/TOUCH INPUT)
The brain receives information about the properties of objects through the skin receptors for tactile information. Based on the properties of touch, with reference to light touch, deep pressure and temperature, we either calm or alert the brain. The repetitive action of manipulating fiddle toys, such as stress balls, has a regula-tory effect on the brain. We literally fiddle to focus. This is exactly what we do when we doodle during phone calls, meetings or conferences. The brain is using a different action to maintain arousal levels. This form of self-regulation is often referred to as using 'brain toys'.
- *Fidgeting and holding objects:* Stress balls, squish balls, paper clips, straws, elastics, pipe cleaners
- *Temperature variables:* Warm baths, cool showers, neutral warmth (being held by another, snuggle under blankets)
- *Light touch:* Tickling, light back scratching, petting a dog or cat, sleep-ing under flannel sheets
- *Deep touch:* Deep 'bear hugs', deep massage, heavy blankets.

Inappropriate/unhealthy strategies
Destructive and invasive touch.

LOOK (VISUAL INPUT)
The retina of the eyes take in all the visual information within our worlds and the brain processes this sensory information for us in order to visually perceive and relate to our surroundings. Visual information can be bombarding and too alerting for the brain, but by manipulating our visual surroundings we can create a calming effect on the brain and body.
- *Variations in light:* Natural lighting versus fluorescent lighting, dim lighting versus bright lighting
- *Variations in colour:* Walls painted a bright colour versus a pastel colour, bulletin boards decorated with bright red, orange, yellow versus muted

brown, beige and old-rose colours
- *Variations in amount of visual distractions:* Visually cluttered versus sparsely decorated room. Busy versus blank screen savers for PCs
- *Visual calmers:* Fish tanks, aquariums, lava lamps.

Inappropriate/unhealthy strategies

Pornography, aggressive and violent visual materials.

LISTEN (AUDITORY INPUT)

Sound has powerful calming or alerting properties and can be used for self-regulation in different forms, intensities and variations to change the arousal level of the brain. Through our ears we hear and experience our worlds.
- *Variation in noise level:* Loud music versus quiet music, screaming versus whispering voices
- *Variation in rhythm:* Fast versus slow music, arhythmical versus rhythmical music
- *Variation in amount of auditory distractions:* Quiet working environment versus noisy environment, sudden unexpected sounds versus constant background noise such as a clock ticking, white noise
- *Auditory calmers:* Sound of running water, water fountains, sea and wave sounds, birdsong.

Inappropriate/unhealthy methods

Excessively loud music.

Take five – the time element

When you consider your need to take five and take a break, you also need to consider time limits. How much time do you allow yourself to self-regulate and how regularly? Is it
- five seconds
- five minutes
- 55 minutes
- five hours
- five days
- five weeks
- five months
- five years?

The *five-second* break is literally taking your attention off your work or task for a few seconds. It could be taking a deep breath or briefly closing your eyes. We tap into this time frame with regular intervals throughout the day. Since the brain can focus and organize optimally for short periods of time only, it is vital briefly to shift focus from your work from time to time. A period often cited in literature is that brain capacity for focus and sustained attention is about 20-40 minutes at a time; it does, however, vary from person to person and situation to situation. The five-second break could therefore be applied once every 20-40 minutes.

The *five-minute* break is usually your quick bathroom breaks or getting up to get a cup of coffee. I guess these could be seen as the nature-call breaks and they are also evident throughout the day. I always advocate drinking lots of water throughout the day since it is such a basic health strategy. The added advantage is a regularly full bladder, which forces one to get up and go to the bathroom. The act of moving is in itself a self-regulation strategy which refocuses the brain. The five-minute break can be replaced by a 15-minute tea break twice a day.

The *55-minute* break is traditionally your lunch break. How many of you have lunch at your desk in front of your PC? It seems to be a general trend I have observed working with adults in the workplace. You may be telling yourself or thinking that you are taking a break, but in actual fact you are maintaining sensory input and your path to sensory overload will accelerate! Taking a quiet lunch break away from your desk is necessary and healthy in order to reduce your climbing arousal level and curb sensory overload.

The *five-hour* break is the shortened version of night-time sleep. I am not advocating five hours sleep, although I guess it seems to be the trend as we get older. A solid 6-8 hours of sleep is necessary for all of us in order to shut down our sensory systems for recharging for the following day. Many people would disagree with me, insisting that you can do with less sleep. That might be true for a while, but in the long term it will affect and increase sensory overload and shutdown and affect your health and general wellness. If you power-nap during the day you may convince me otherwise …

The *five-day* break is a short holiday or long weekend taken at certain times throughout the year. It is especially worthwhile following times of increased stress or prior to major events. It is useful for maintaining a sense of equilibrium throughout the whole year.

The *five-week* break is supposed to form part of your annual leave or holiday break. Where or when you do this is beside the point, but the value of taking an extended break cannot be over-emphasized for us living in this fast-paced, crazy world! This is the time of the year where we read the books we never get to, watch the movies we never have time for, take our daily walks on the beach and spend quality time with our loved ones.

The *five-month* break is for those who are lucky enough to be semi-retired and work for certain times of the year while taking off other times of the year. I personally don't know many people in this position, and if anyone knows the secret of how to get here, please let me know.

The *five-year* break is an extended sabbatical even more scarce than the five month break. Probably very few of us are in a position to take a five-year break, to leave behind our roles, work and responsibilities and just relax. I guess that could be considered real retirement. Retirement should be seen as a positive and productive stage, that can be shorter or longer than five years. Although a potentially difficult transition for the workaholics, it is the ability to sit back and relax after spending your prime years earning a living and working hard.

The point I am trying to make is that taking a break, and taking all these time breaks, (including the five-year break if you can afford it) will ensure a less stressed world. Using the take five self-regulation strategies, together with your time elements, will ensure you maintain the best state of arousal, manage your stress, and prevent sensory overload, shutdown and the related burn-out.

It will improve health and wellness, increase productivity and raise work performance levels.

To Lisa Katzeff
Thank you for letting me into your beautiful home when I needed time, peace, quiet and inspiration to finish the last few chapters.

To Helené Bestbier
Thank you for your contribution to anticipation, planning and preparation.

CHAPTER 7

Sensory intelligent self-care

"The easiest step towards improving the quality of life consists of simply learning to control the body and its senses." (Mihaly Csikszentmihalyi, *Flow: the psychology of optimal experience*)

This quote is the best and truest reflection I could find to introduce the concept of sensory intelligent self-care. Our senses create and facilitate our responses, behaviours and actions on a daily basis. It is the process through which we learn, act, communicate and work. However, these are also the channels through which we experience sensory overload and stress and our lives start spinning out of control. When this happens, get back to basics, take up the senses, de-stress and recharge.

It sounds simple, but in practice is a lot harder to implement. Life's school is hard and demanding. It is as if we cannot or won't believe that we deserve the effort and energy to create the necessary 'me'-time. Me-time is all too often seen as selfish and unnecessary by a large group of our population, especially working mothers. What a pity! It is through quality and efficient me-time that we gain control, recharge our batteries and become the people we want to be.

To find a base for intervention we will look at the PEO (person-environment-occupation) model as well as the EHP (Ecology of human performance) model. Both these models provide a powerful framework in creating the best intervention strategies and approaches.

The PEO model

There is a complex and dynamic relationship between people, environments and occupations. Mary Law put these together as the PEO model in 1996, stating that the specific interaction between them will be a facilitator of our performance. Research has produced extensive proof that performance is shaped by a dynamic interdependence between persons, occupations and environments. Although the general world typically thinks of occupations as being work, it is actually a far broader concept in the context of occupational therapy and practice, and has been defined thus: "Occupations are ... clusters of activities and tasks in which people engage while carrying out various roles in multiple environments" (Strong, *et al*, 1999).

By considering sensory elements within an environment and the roles of occupation for a particular individual the model is a valuable tool for intervention from a sensory perspective. In this context *person* includes sensory profile, interests and values; *environment* includes sensory elements within the environment, physical structures and characteristics, resources, social factors and friends; occupation includes *work*, self-care, life roles, social responsibility; and *occupational performance* refers to the success and efficiency of tasks completed for our life roles.

In the PEO model three overlapping circles represent the three main dimensions, namely person, occupation and environment. The overlap in the centre represents the occupational performance of the individual or the person. The greater the overlap, the better the fit with resultant increased occupational performance. The opposite is also true: the smaller the overlap, the poorer the fit and the weaker the occupational performance.

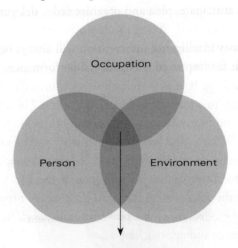

Occupational performance

When the environment is not a good fit for the individual from a sensory perspective, occupational performance will be diminished. A good example could typically be a sensory defensive individual working in a noisy open-plan office environment. His or her performance is likely to be affected because there is poor goodness-of-fit.

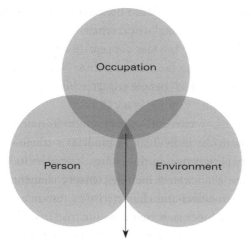

Reduced occupational performance

Intervention strategies would then be based on the:
- Person: self-regulation strategies, sensory diets, desensitization
- Environment: making changes to the environment to reduce sensory overload
- Occupation: anticipate, plan and organize tasks, delegate or adapt tasks.

The aim with sensory intelligence intervention will always be to create a positive goodness-of-fit for improved occupational performance.

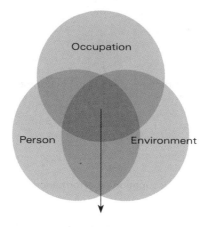

Greater occupational performance

In summary, applying the PEO model is necessary for obtaining an optimum goodness-of-fit between the individual's sensory profile, the sensory environment and the task demands. We will now discuss the different approaches to addressing these three important components.

The EHP model of intervention

The EHP (Ecology of human performance) model is an intervention model developed by Winnie Dunn in 1999. It provides a framework to assist us in identifying multiple intervention approaches. It enables us to look at the bigger picture. Human behaviour is complex. Humans operate in different and unique environments, which contribute to their behaviours, actions, habits, likes and dislikes. From research we know that the interaction between individuals and their environment affects their behaviour and performance. How do we get the individual and the environment together? Through the senses! We all have different roles to play in life. Therefore, we need to consider all possible variables when identifying the best-fit strategies from a sensory perspective. When I work with individual clients I address all these intervention alternatives. Although the emphasis may shift from person to person, considering each component would ensure the best results. In other words, when you want to be more sensory intelligent in order to take care of your own sensory needs, make sure you assess your life from all these perspectives, and find possibilities in all of them for better health and wellness.

The following diagram provides you with the basic outline before we discuss each component separately:

Combining the EHP model (Dunn) and PEO model (Law) for optimum intervention

Intervention alternatives	What?	PEO	How?
Establish/ Restore	Challenge personal thresholds	P	Develop or improve skills of the individual: desensitization, brushing, therapeutic sensory strategies, sound therapy, alternative therapies, skills development
Alter	Change environmental context	E	Interventions that change context of tasks or environment
Adapt	Job, home and environment	O/E	Creating the best fit or match between person and tasks, sensory ergonomics
Prevent	Avoid potential overload	P/O	Avoid potential situations associated with sensory overload and shutdown Avoiding strategies Planning and anticipation Time and organizational management
Create	Self-regulation strategies Sensory diets	P	To achieve optimal arousal in times of sensory stress, respiration and breathing techniques Introduce regular activities to address sensory needs

Establish or restore: challenge personal thresholds

Since our genes and the way we were brought up determine our sensory thresholds, can we really change them? Can you teach your body and brain to be less sensitive to noise, or touch, or movement when you are a root? Can you teach your body to not need so much movement, or olfactory stimulation when you are a leaf? This is a difficult question and I've searched for the answer through many gurus in our field of practice. I have had to come up with my own answer.

A threshold is not a specific point; it is a band that fluctuates a little. Some days we are more sensitive or seeking than others.

In our work with children using sensory integration therapy we succeed in making subtle changes to thresholds. Children's brains are still maturing and there is more plasticity to work with. We also concentrate on teaching them the skills they need in order to function. Plasticity in the brain is evident until the day we die, so yes, we can make changes throughout life.

DESENSITIZATION

In adults desensitizing the senses remains more tricky and difficult. I mostly use this component with adults with low threshold, the roots. Sensation seekers don't seem to have the motivation to lower their thresholds, but sensation avoiders often seem to want to increase their thresholds so that their sensitivity has a reduced impact.

There are two important questions to ask when addressing the senses through this intervention approach:

- How much is your sensory sensitivity, sensory avoiding, low registration or sensation seeking affecting your life?
- How motivated are you to make the necessary changes?

If the answer to the first question is 'a lot', and the answer to the next question is 'yes', then read further.

Challenging your thresholds would mean that you literally will be exposing your body and brain to sensory input for which you are sensitive. If you are touch sensitive, it is more touch that you need. If you are movement sensitive, it is movement that you need. I only recommend that you challenge your thresholds this way when you are in a good space, and when you are seriously motivated to do so.

If you are movement sensitive for the vestibular system and you go on a roller-coaster ride 99 times, I guess your brain will then start to habituate. It will get use to the feeling of this processing pathway in your brain and tolerate the 100th ride with reduced stress. I don't particularly like movement stimulation and I tend to get car sick. My vestibular system does not seem to allow me to go crazy with head movement. Do I want to go on a roller-coaster ride 99 times to desensitize? No way. It is just not important to me. This emphasizes the importance of motivation.

Andrea*, a 40-year-old female with sensory sensitivity, especially in the mouth area, disliked certain food textures and would gag when having to eat certain food types. She was distressed that this excluded her and her husband from being invited to dinner parties. She was avoided as she was labelled as picky and fussy. For Andrea it was important to get rid of this label and I recommended that she tried new foods in the safety of her own home. There it is okay to spit it out. The brain's ability to habituate was used here so that she could desensitize her taste and smell systems through continued exposure. It did improve significantly. Andrea would never be an adventurous eater, but managed to eat many things she had always avoided before.

THE BRUSHING PROTOCOL

This is a specific and specialized treatment, developed by Patricia Willbarger, an occupational therapist in the USA and widely used by occupational therapists across the world in the sensory integration field. Our skin is our largest sensory organ, connected to the brain by our nervous system and governed by our brain. The sensory systems feed information from our environment, through sense receptors, and neural impulses via our nervous system, directly to the brain. The brain then organizes it, sends it back through the nervous system for use in understanding, adaptation, learning, and skill development. The brushing protocol involves deep pressure, brushing the skin with a very specific non-scratching brush, followed by gentle joint compression to send information to the brain in an organized fashion. Simply put, it primes the brain to receive and organize information in an effective and useful way. It is done approximately every two hours for a specified number of days and then according to the needs of the individual. Consistency is a critical factor. It has proven especially helpful in sensory defensiveness. It reduces defensive behaviours and sensory overload. Although developed and mostly used for children, I do recommend this therapy to some of my clients. This protocol is always considered to be a part of a more comprehensive occupational therapy treatment plan and should only be used under the supervision and guidance of a registered occupational therapist. Using this technique without instruction from a trained therapist could be harmful at worst, and useless at best.

This is a powerful tool in sensory integration therapy, but it is specialized, specific and takes a great deal of effort and discipline to maintain the process correctly.

Didi*, a 36-year old advocate from Johannesburg, started using the brushing protocol on a regular basis to treat her severe sensory defensiveness. After I taught her to brush herself and apply joint compression, she started using the therapy daily. She had three brushes that she kept in convenient places. She often had to brush herself in the bathroom at work as well. Her feedback was that when she brushed five times per day, she was a lot more composed, her sensory overload decreased and she was more productive. Sometimes she only managed to brush herself three times per day. This also worked well, but increased arousal levels and sensory overload were then more prevalent. And I know she was telling the truth – I had to replace her brushes regularly.

THERAPEUTIC SENSORY STRATEGIES

It is possible to desensitize the brain and nervous system by performing movement, vibration and deep-pressure touch therapy. Kinnealy and Pfeiffer (see page 191) did a study on the treatment of sensory defensiveness by introducing a series of sensory activities for their therapeutic value. Clients had to perform regular self-treatment by engaging in the suggested activities over a period of one month. The treatment protocol incorporated proprioception, vestibular and deep-pressure touch. These three systems are known in the field of sensory integration to have a modulatory and organizing effect on the brain. The equipment used was a therapy ball, rocking chair, brushing, air pillow, trampoline, platform swing, vibrator and mat. After treatment participants showed reduced levels of sensory defensiveness and anxiety.

SOUND THERAPY

Music and sound were first used for their therapeutic value by French physician Dr Alfred Tomatis. Many other approaches developed out of his work and occupational therapists are now combining sound therapy with sensory integration therapy with great success. Sound and movement work together beautifully, owing to the neurological proximity between the auditory (hearing) and the vestibular (inner ear balance and movement) systems. They lie right next to each other and also share the same nerve (electrical wire) to get information to the cortex.

Sound waves with frequencies of between 500 and 4000 Hz are being processed for speech and language. Frequencies below 750 Hz are basically processed via the vestibular system in the form of vibration and perceived via the 'body'. This combination is particularly useful in sensory integration therapy. Sound therapy entails a series of listening exercises through headphones to prime the brain for auditory and vestibular information, which reduce auditory sensitivity. Because of the neural interconnections with most of the other sensory systems general sensitivity across all systems are often reduced.

SKILLS DEVELOPMENT

We all have barriers and weaknesses that can potentially affect how we function. We are never too old to learn and neuro-plasticity indicates that our brains can learn and develop until the day we die. With skills development I refer to activities such as doing a time-management course when sensory overload tends to throw you off guard and you struggle to cope. Learning to manage your time with the use of strategies could be a useful supplement to attending to your sensory needs as well. You might have difficulty with relationships: conflict management courses could then be useful. There are hundreds of possibilities when we consider skills development. In addition to the ones I've mentioned, other possibilities are telephone skills, computer skills, parenting skills, cooking skills, organizational skills, etc. These are ways to improve your skills as an individual so that you can cope with the demands of your life more effectively and with less stress.

Alter: change environmental context

Considering a change in context is often quite extensive, significant and life changing. This could refer to changing your job, profession, moving house or office, getting married, getting divorced, relocating or retiring. These are real, significant changes we make in life. Although this is territory where I tread very carefully and often lie awake at night when it becomes part of my intervention process while coaching a client, it is inevitable in some cases.

In Didi's* case, she and her husband got divorced partly because they were so sensory incompatible. However, a breakdown can be the result of sensory issues in combination with other relationship problems. The fact that Didi was now alone in her home environment, without the 'noise' of her rock musician husband did reduce Didi's stress and overload. I did support Didi's decision to give up her office in chambers in the middle of Johannesburg and move to a home office. This was another contextual change (I much rather preferred) that contributed to her sensory needs positively. Her environment was then more conducive to optimal performance as she did not have to commute so much any more, the surrounding noise and activity levels were reduced significantly and she had the security of her own home environment.

Stacey* is a client I will be introducing to you again in the next chapter regarding work place issues. She is a real root with general sensory sensitivity, and worked in an open-plan office environment. Now, there are open-plan office environments that are set up well and can be conducive to good performance by the roots in our society. But then there are other open-plan office environments that are really badly set up, probably owing to financial constraints rather than lack of knowledge. Stacey was working in the latter kind of environment. We worked through many changes and introduced many strategies for her, but eventually she did resign from her position and left the company. She needed to change her context in order to meet her sensory needs and ensure optimum performance, but also to be happy and contented.

I would advise anyone to consider all aspects of themselves and their environment before making contextual changes. However, the benefits of obtaining the optimum goodness-of-fit environment and place for you in society should override the fear of making the changes. In many cases this strategy assists individuals in finding their passions, enjoying work and life and living it to the fullest. Change is difficult but often inevitable!

Adapt work and home environments

Creating the best fit between person, occupation and environment is an easy and manageable component. It still surprises me that individuals rarely identify the sensory stressors within their environments. They know that a particular situation is difficult for them, but the sensory connections are rarely made. Changing the task or environment so that sensory irritations are reduced when you are a root, or changing to increase sensory input when you are a leaf, is applying what I call *sensory ergonomics*.

Sensory refers to sensation; that aspect of consciousness resulting from the stimulation of a nerve process beginning at any point in the body and passing through the brain, especially by those stimuli affecting any of the sense organs, such as hearing, taste, touch, smell, sight and movement.

Ergonomics refers to the study of the relationship between an individual and his or her environment, with special reference to anatomical, physiological and psychological factors.

Sensory ergonomics can therefore be defined as the act of manipulating an environment through either adding or withdrawing sensory stimuli to meet the needs of the individual functioning within that environment.

In our context *sensory ergonomics* refers to changes and/or adaptations within a current physical, structured environment to help an individual achieve an optimal level of arousal and performance. It is applicable to both home and work environments. It is the subtle changes that you can make within your living and/or working space to meet your sensory needs.

General sensory ergonomics for roots (reduce sensory input)

Smell/Taste	• Contain smells and tastes
	• Use a humidifier to control air flow, smells and toxins
Visual	• Reduce clutter
	• Create clean and organized spaces (files, drawers, cupboards, shelves)
	• Maintain good filing habits
	• Use full-spectrum or natural lighting
	• Switch off the lights
	• Close curtains and/or blinds
	• Use a blank screen saver on your PC

Touch	• Move seating away from air conditioner outflow, fan or open windows
	• Close windows to prevent heavy air flow
	• Maintain a constant temperature within your living or working space
	• When in a lift, stand at the back, or right at the control panel with your back against the wall
Auditory	• Turn down volume on telephone
	• Put cellphone on mute/vibrate
	• Change ring tones
	• Turn the radio/TV down or off
	• Use visual instead of auditory instructions
	• Use white noise or calming, repetitive sounds that help to drown out other distracting auditory elements
	• Try to position noisy electronic devices as far away from you as possible
Movement	• Use the stairs rather than escalators
	• Place the objects you need most regularly within arm's reach at your desk to reduce having to bend down and move a lot
	• Organize your kitchen for easy access to reduce excessive movement
Activity level	• Plan and organize tasks sequentially
	• Put materials that you need in a sequential order
	• Schedule your day according to your typical arousal and stress levels; often it means doing the demanding, difficult tasks in the morning, leaving the mundane tasks for later in the day

General sensory ergonomics for leaves (add sensory input)

Smell/Taste	• Burn scented candles, incense, etc.
	• Chew or suck on peppermints
Visual	• Use bright lighting
	• Switch on the lights
	• Use colours and contrasts in home or workspace
	• Organized clutter can work for you
	• Use a moving screen saver on your PC
	• When sitting in a group, position yourself facing the door or in the middle of the group
	• Open blinds/curtains
	• Re-arrange furniture regularly

Touch	• Use different textures in the home and office
	• Open windows
	• Walk barefoot
Auditory	• Use background noise
	• Put on the radio/TV/music while working
	• Attend activities where lots of auditory stimuli are present
Movement	• Use cordless phones to walk and talk
	• Sit on a therapy ball when working – it allows more movement opportunities
	• Position needed objects in such a way that you have to get up and walk to get them
Activity level	• Incorporate novelty
	• Change the way in which you do tasks
	• Work in groups
	• Socialize regularly
	• Change your seating and/or working positions

Prevent: avoid potential sensory overload

This component of intervention is particularly relevant to low threshold roots. Knowing your sensory stressors is crucial to be able to avoid situations potentially associated with sensory overload and shutdown. It is also the one component that individuals do implement more subconsciously. You won't find roots going to a busy shopping mall on a Saturday morning; they would rather go in the week when it is quieter. It is also unlikely that you would find them at the upcoming rock concert, the local fair/bazaar/expo or show. They instinctively know to avoid crowded, busy, loud and colourful places. The reality is that sometimes these places cannot be avoided by roots. Then it is a matter of planning and preparing so that they can cope with these environments successfully.

AVOIDING STRATEGIES

Sensory ergonomics is changing the environment or tasks when having to cope with a particular place or an environment, whether you like it or not. Avoiding strategies entail developing an awareness of which sensory events are likely to create overload and avoiding them altogether. There are some overlaps between avoiding strategies and sensory ergonomics.

Smell/Taste	• Apply smell/taste sensory ergonomics
	• Avoid wearing perfume, scented products, fragrant candles
	• Avoid smelly places (i.e. fish shops, perfume shops)
	• Choose familiar restaurants and food choices
Visual	• Wear sunglasses
	• Decorate with a less is more approach
	• Use soft and gentle colours
	• Avoid and remove clutter
Touch	• When in a group setting, sit with your back to a wall, at the end of the table, if possible in a place where the chances of being touched are minimized
	• When standing in a line, carry a backpack or hold your bag behind your body to minimize unexpected touch from behind
	• Use gloves when working with food, gardening, or handling messy objects
Auditory	• Avoid busy, crowded places
	• Commute at times when it is less crowded and noisy
	• Avoid working in busy, crowded, tight, open-plan spaces
	• Socialize in small groups with familiar people
Movement	• Avoid amusement parks – or be a spectator rather than a participant
	• Avoid long car or boat trips
Activity level	• Plan and organize tasks sequentially before doing them
	• Mentally prepare yourself for transitions
	• Avoid traffic and congested areas; try to commute outside of peak hours
	• Shop in small, organized shops at quiet times

ANTICIPATION, PLANNING AND PREPARATION (APP)

We need to anticipate activities and situations in daily life which tend to over-load us, tap our energy and result in stress. The reality is that it is often the mundane day-to-day tasks that result in sensory overload, stress and shutdown. So if we approach these potentially stressful situations with a plan in place and prepare ourselves, we seem to cope better. We reduce sensory overload, perform better, get more done and feel more in control of the situation. In my work with both children and adults, the careful anticipation, planning and preparation of daily tasks and especially transitions, have proven highly beneficial and success-ful, especially for roots.

The APP process is based on the arousal theories with special reference to the arousal curve and sensory events over time, which tend to increase our arousal levels.

If we take any sensory event, for example washing dishes, feeding the children, having an important meeting, travelling by plane to a conference, visiting friends, going to a birthday party, the APP process will consist of three main stages:

Before the event • The event itself • After the event

Each of these stages consists of a further three sub-stages to help with planning and preparation.

- *Before the event:* Aware – Orientate – Organize
- *The event itself:* Contact – Action – Complete
- *After the event:* Withdraw – Depart – Rest

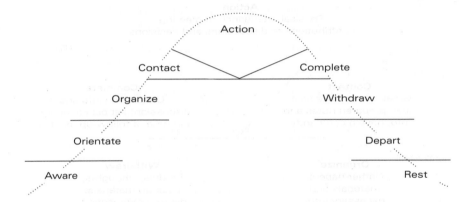

Before the event
Aware: Knowledge and information about a particular event long in advance is important. We need to know in order to prepare. Last-minute and unexpected demands are often difficult to cope with.

Orientate: This is the top-down inhibition approach that we use to mentally prepare ourselves for a particular task, activity or situation.

Organize: Gathering all possible information and starting to form a goal and plan on how we will approach the necessary task.

The event itself
Contact: Initiating and beginning the task or situation. It would mean a gradual, systematic approach to the task.

Action: Performing the task itself.

Completion: Closing or completion stage of a task.

After the event
Withdraw: Mentally withdrawing from the task or situation.

Depart: Physically withdrawing from the task or situation. Evaluate and reflect on outcomes.

Rest: Using a self-regulation strategy to reduce arousal and calm the senses.

If we apply the APP process in practice, it will look like the example below when using it with a multi-sensory event of attending an important meeting. Each stage can also have a time limit put to it, depending on the context and situation. It can be utilized across numerous situations and events and should be customized to fit your particular needs.

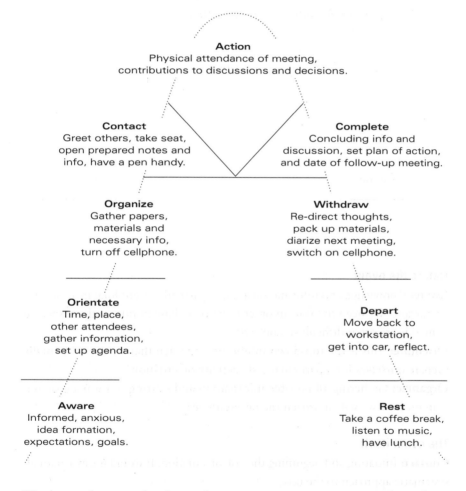

Action
Physical attendance of meeting,
contributions to discussions and decisions.

Contact
Greet others, take seat,
open prepared notes and
info, have a pen handy.

Complete
Concluding info and
discussion, set plan of action,
and date of follow-up meeting.

Organize
Gather papers,
materials and
necessary info,
turn off cellphone.

Withdraw
Re-direct thoughts,
pack up materials,
diarize next meeting,
switch on cellphone.

Orientate
Time, place,
other attendees,
gather information,
set up agenda.

Depart
Move back to
workstation,
get into car, reflect.

Aware
Informed, anxious,
idea formation,
expectations, goals.

Rest
Take a coffee break,
listen to music,
have lunch.

We also need to consider that we have numerous events occurring throughout a normal day. Depending on the importance or overload potential of each situation, you can decide for which events you want to use this approach. A normal day for a working mother could potentially look like this:

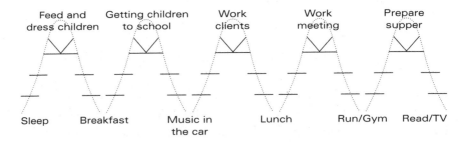

I am being very optimistic with that run/gym break after work. It is often virtually impossible for working mothers to get to do exercise during that time of the day. It often will be done at 6 in the morning. And there is the final event of putting children to bed, which should be added to the event curves.

The work curve could consist of numerous other small tasks that could individually be performed through the APP process:

The work phase:

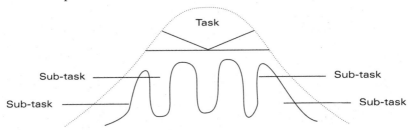

This could potentially consist of meeting with a particular client, e-mail contacts, meeting with suppliers, drawing up advertising material, etc.

Whatever your role or position in life is, whether you are single, married, working or not working, you will be able to curve your own events based on your work, home and social responsibility. Remember even an activity as mundane as washing the dishes can be analysed using the APP principle. You also might find some situations or events more difficult and important than others. You are likely to benefit from using the APP principles with those tricky situations.

It may appear to be a long and laborious process, which might take some time and effort to get used to. With frequent repetition, this becomes a natural process of organization and will assist you in getting through difficult events and situations. It has been a most helpful strategy for many low threshold roots and my experience has been that roots are drawn to its principles.

Time and organizational management

Since sensory overload and related stress are such a reality in life, the importance of time and organizational management cannot be stressed enough. It is a fact that some of us are just more organized than others, and some of us always seem to manage to squeeze one more hour out of the day than others. Basic principles of managing time optimally and creating as much organization as possible are crucial to maintain a sense of order and prevent sensory overload.

I am no specialist when it comes to the area of time management and organization but do know and apply the general rules. I do refer some of my clients to a professional organizer should it be necessary. Basic time management principles are:

- Use a diary. Plan your day, week, month and year
- Be pro-active, do what needs to be done
- Avoid procrastination
- Set your clock for 15-30 minutes earlier in the morning if you tend to run late. Running late at the start of your day often sets a negative trend that seems to continue throughout your day
- If you tend to be late on a regular basis, set your watch 2-3 minutes later. It helps to hurry you along
- Set pockets of time aside for some activities, and move on when that time is up, whether you have completed them or not
- Try to establish which activities during your day take the most amount of your time. See if you can cut that down
- Work according to a schedule, a structure, a system; the more systematic your systems are, the better you'll function. This is what the Information Technology industry is all about, isn't it? Every personal computer and related program seems to run systems for organization, planning your day, lists and actions
- Say no; you cannot do it all! Don't overload yourself!
- Don't try to do too much within a day. Doing less more thoroughly is preferable to doing more in a hasty, inefficient and incomplete manner
- Get help. Delegate. Get a personal assistant, a baby sitter, a granny to help, or a friend, whoever is available. I think we have fallen into a not-asking-for-help culture. It is through helping one another that we save time and reduce overload
- Apply the anticipation, planning and preparation technique.

Basic organizational principles are:
- Declutter, declutter, declutter!
- Create spaces where you function, work and do tasks efficiently that are conducive to your personal needs
- Prioritize and set clear goals for yourself
- Throw away unwanted stuff, papers, old documents, etc.
- Introduce and maintain an efficient filing system

- Create spaces, folders, files, baskets, etc. to organize your documents or materials. Mark them clearly
- Clean up on a regular basis
- Keep and maintain a diary, whether it is a paper one, or an electronic one. And use it!
- Apply the anticipation, planning and preparation technique.

Create self-regulation strategies and sensory diets

Self-regulation strategies – sensory snacks

TAKE FIVE, TAKE A BREAK! Self-regulation strategies are used to achieve optimal arousal in times of sensory stress. These are quick, fast and easily accessible activities that we use continuously throughout the day to maintain arousal and focus, therefore the verbal label: sensory snacks. Please refer to Chapter 6 for a detailed discussion on the principles of self-regulation strategies.

Respiration and breathing techniques are a further useful tool for self-regulation. Although not necessarily sensory based from outside the body, they provide an internal sense of control and calm. Deep breathing unconsciously reduces stress and creates a feeling of relaxation as it forces a deeper control onto the body.

Sensory diets – sensory meals

Sensory diets are activities to introduce into your daily living to meet your sensory needs in a more prolonged manner. Together with self-regulation strategies they form the backbone of stress management through the senses. A sensory diet includes the activities we do outside of work and home responsibilities. It is nurturing our sensory needs through the use of exercise, social activities, creative outlets, and other activities in which we participate that are enjoyable. We call it *sensory meals* since we spend a little bit more time and effort on them than on self-regulation strategies.

Everyone should be engaged in physical exercise activities to keep fit, meet with friends for social gatherings and introduce activities to facilitate self-expression and which are creative outlets. Obviously the type, intensity and frequency of your choices will be dependent on your sensory needs, sensory overload occurrences and lifestyle choices.

What do you do outside of home and work responsibilities that you love doing that charges your batteries, that makes you feel relaxed?

Do you exercise, do art, pottery, gardening, attend book clubs, garden clubs, play cards, braai with friends? When we introduce a meaningful and regular sensory diet in our lives, it calms the senses, stimulates the mind, controls sensory overload and stress and make us happy individuals.

Refer back to your sensory systems checklist, in Chapter 3 to identify your best-fit options for sensory diets. The possibilities are endless:

Sensory diet possibilities
Movement foods
Also refer to the movement system for analysis of the properties of movement tasks to fit your particular sensory profile.

> Weight training; Running: road running, trail running; Contact sport: rugby, wrestling, karate, boxing; Scuba diving; Swimming; Surfing; Water-skiing; Gardening; Rowing; Walking; Dancing: belly dancing, pole dancing, tango dancing, Latin dancing, salsa, etc.; Roller-coaster rides; Sky diving, parachuting; Flying airplanes; Adventure clubs; Hiking; Beach volleyball; Rollerblading; Rock climbing; Fishing; Cricket; Tennis; Gym: aerobics, weight-training; Biking: road racing, mountain biking

Tactile foods
> Social clubs; Massage ; Sitting on a bean bag chair; Playing a musical instrument; Gardening; Pottery; Sculpting

Visual foods
> Reading; TV; Decorating; Art; Quilt making; Needle work and embroidery (strong movement component as well); Visiting museums, art galleries, flea markets, festivals

Sound foods
> Music; Playing musical instruments; Drumming; Concerts

Smell/Taste foods
> Cooking; Attending cooking classes and demonstrations; Aromatherapy; Wine tasting; Food and wine festivals

Combination foods
> Breathing; Progressive and other relaxation techniques; Yoga; Pilates; The Alexander techniques; Rolfing; Tai Chi; Feng Shui; Meditation, etc.

The above listed activities were grouped according to the sense they would stimulate the most. All of them have multi-sensory elements. The interactive wiring for all the senses in the brain makes it virtually impossible to dissociate one sense completely from another. However, working through the above choices (and there are obviously many others) you will most certainly find an activity that appeals to you.

A regular sensory diet is crucial for us to manage our sensory overload and stress levels. It calms and organizes the brain and body and creates a healthy and happy lifestyle.

To David Crow and other leaders in corporate industry who think like him.
Thank you for not only believing but also investing in human capital.

CHAPTER 8

Sensory intelligence in the workplace

Sensory intelligence is important in all aspects of life including our participation in a daily working role. No matter what your job description, you have certain expectations to fulfil, whether company directed or self-created.

Using sensory intelligence in the work place will add significant value to your performance, productivity and team cohesion. The application of sensory intelligence has value and benefit with regards to recruitment, staff training and development. Sensory intelligence is a primitive, automatic, yet unexplored part of who we are. This relationship between us and our environment is a facilitator for how we work, function and interact.

Human capital

The concept of *human capital* caught me by surprise. Deep down as an occupational therapist I firmly believe in people. After all, in the field of human sciences the importance and value of the person remains the core in any equation. Initially, being naïve and treading in unknown territory, the lavish use of the term *human capital* created a sense of enthusiasm that was somewhat misplaced. I had to learn very quickly that the bottom line monetary benefits remain the first priority of any business. Rightfully so, that's how we stay in business! However, investment in the wellness and productivity of your work force does increase the bottom line. Taking the best possible care of your workforce will ensure optimum productivity and draw the best talent – on your way to becoming an employer of choice while creating optimal value for your shareholders.

In today's highly competitive business environment, any company worth its salt does everything in its power to improve bottom-line earnings. Competitive advantage in industry today depends on operational efficiency based on information technology with systems, structures and procedures developed to the fullest. Since people have to make this happen, there are more work expectations of staff, with higher workloads and tighter deadlines. People are expected to produce work of higher quality in shorter time frames.

The bottom line is that we operate in busy, sensory overloaded environments, often not optimally suited to their work roles. It creates stress that reduces productivity, results in absenteeism, stress-related illnesses and attrition – quite the opposite of what management should aspire to achieve with the concept of building human capital.

The corporate wellness-industry is said to be one of the fastest growing industries in the world. Is that true for us in South Africa? I have some reservations since I have had a lot of contact with decision makers in business who merely seem to be paying lip service to developing human capital. Enthusiasm for the concept of corporate wellness is shared by a select few. Research across the world confirms that stress in the workplace affects businesses extensively. Through its impact on productivity, it exerts pressure on profit margins and has negative spin-offs on families and communities – something that will come back to haunt organizations. Absenteeism is contributing to huge visible losses in industry. But it is the invisible losses resulting from reduced productivity that can potentially cost a company dearly. Until such time that we can objectively measure the monetary impact of poor health and other consequences of the misfit of individuals to their job and environment, these losses will not be fully appreciated.

How can sensory intelligence be used to improve this situation?

Your senses at work

There seems to be a general ignorance of the impact of the senses on daily living for most individuals and groups that I've worked with thus far. Reconnecting to the senses within your environment is important to increase awareness and facilitate this insight. I created the table below to illustrate how your senses are bombarded in a general office environment. It will obviously differ from one environment to the next, but this table covers the basics.

Noise and sounds interpreted by the auditory channel	• Electronic noise • Faxes, phones, computers • Air conditioners • Pitch and volume of human voices
Visual input interpreted by the visual channel	• Lights, contrasts, reflections • People and activities in your visual field • Clutter • Paperwork • Computer screen savers
Touch input interpreted by the tactile channel	• Touch and proximity of others in your personal space • Stepping into a crowded lift • Feeling of clothing textures, jewellery or hair and skin
Movement input interpreted by the inner ear and body sense channels	• Walking in your office building or other related work areas • Using stairs, escalators, lifts • Commute: driving car/taxi/bus • Sitting still and concentrate
Smell and taste interpreted by the nose and tongue channels	• Odours in immediate environment • Chemical smells • Food smells and tastes • Smell of lotions, perfumes • Body odours
Multi-sensory processing	• Work routines • Concentration • Preference for quiet subdued or busy environments • Interpersonal relationships with co-workers • Handling change and unexpected events • Time management • Organizational skills • Stress management • Frustration tolerance • Learning and studying

Customizing sensory intelligence for the workplace

When we apply sensory intelligence in the workplace, everything thus far covered in the book is carefully considered for any work environment. The principles can be used successfully to recruit the best individual for a position, for the development and training of staff and also for the best placement of people. The sensory profile quadrant descriptions for the work place can be summarized as follows:

Low registration	Sensation seeking
These individuals have a high tolerance for environmental stimuli. *They react passively to their environment:*	These individuals have a high tolerance for environmental stimuli. *They react actively to their environment:*
• Are able to focus in distracting, noisy and busy environments • Can miss environmental cues • Might appear uninterested, withdrawn • Are conscientious	• Seek out and create additional environmental stimuli • Are active, 'on the go', continuously engaging • Often multi-task with ease • Are excitable, energetic • Get bored easily, fidgety, distractible
Needs: • Intensified input • Clear instructions repeated both verbally and in writing (e-mail)	Needs: • Activity, variety, novelty and change • Include them in new products or processes; they potentially would enjoy client marketing, travelling, socials with clients
Sensory sensitivity	**Sensation avoiding**
These individuals have a low tolerance for environmental stimuli. *They react passively to their environment:*	These individuals have a low tolerance for environmental stimuli. *They react actively to their environment:*
• Are easily affected by environmental stimuli • Are inclined to get distracted and irritated by the environment • Have a high level of awareness and are 'in tune' with the environment • Can be detail orientated	• Can be overwhelmed or bothered by stimuli • Avoid environmental stimuli or engage to reduce stimuli • Are resistant to change • Rely on rigid rituals to increase predictability • Are good at establishing structure and routine

Needs:

- Less sensory stimuli
- More quiet and controlled environments

Needs:

- Quiet surroundings
- Clear expectations, structure and predictability

Using sensory intelligence for optimal staff placement

Considering the quadrant scores and related behaviours based on the sensory profile, the following can assist in maximizing people potential by attending to their primitive sensory needs. When you analyse specific job descriptions based on what is generally expected of those filling them, the sensory profile allows you to match people optimally to their needs/task/expectations/requirements. The type of tasks required for a particular position as well as the kind of the environments the jobs require can be used to place them in the quadrants.

Please note that this is not considering all possible jobs out there and is just a general best-fit job description. Do not panic if you do not have a match. You can still allow for your sensory needs to be catered for within a current job situation, even though the general job description seems to be contradictory to your needs.

However, if there is a significant miss-fit between your sensory needs and your current work role, you will most probably know it already and the sensory profile might just confirm this for you.

Low registration	Sensation seeking
Best-fit job descriptions:	Best-fit job descriptions:
• Call centre agents	• Tour guides
• Stock traders (especially when working on a trading floor)	• Formula-one racers
• Flea-market sellers	• Pre-school teachers
• Preschool teachers	• Entrepreneurs
• Open-plan office workers	• Open-plan office workers
• Estate agents	• Actors, dancers
• Cabin crew	• Journalists
	• Any job with travelling assignments
	• Sales and marketing
	• Police and rescue personnel

Sensory sensitivity	Sensation avoiding
Best-fit job descriptions:	Best-fit job descriptions:
• Computer programmers	• Lawyers
• High school teachers	• Advocates
• Artists	• Accountants
• Therapists, counsellors, psychologists	• Writers
• Strategists	• Farmers
• Human resource staff	• Systems analysts and developers
• Systems analysts	• Librarians
• Researchers	

The elaboration of job descriptions is important to establish whether you are in tune with your primitive sensory needs. Do bear in mind that you can do a sensation seeking kind of job such as sales when you are more of a sensation avoider. It is then important to structure your sales position in a sequential and predictable way. For instance a true sensation seeker will find cold-call selling easy whereas a sensation avoider as a sales person will approach selling more methodically and systematically, most probably not cold calling.

The job-fits aim primarily at describing the type of job, but the environment also needs to be considered. It is always the best solution to combine your job expectations and environment to fit your sensory profile. Remember the challenge is to match your sensory needs within your current job description. Can you change your job environment or tasks to suit your sensory needs? The processes to adapt your work environment or job to suit your sensory needs are what I call sensory ergonomics. This was also discussed in the previous chapter.

Sensory ergonomics

Sensory ergonomics refers to changes and/or adaptations within a current physical, structured work environment to help an individual achieve an optimal level of arousal and performance. This will ensure optimal alertness for the individual to work productively. It is the subtle changes that you can make within your working space as well as your job demands to meet your sensory needs.

Low registration	Sensation seeking
• Sit close to the speaker at meetings, follow a written agenda	• Sit where you can observe all the action, take notes, or lead the meeting
• Use bright lighting	• Use cordless phones to walk and talk
• Use colours and contrasts in your workspace, label all drawers, cupboards, files	• Incorporate novelty
	• Use colourful spaces and work areas
	• Change the way in which you do tasks
• Use a moving screen saver on your PC	• Work in groups
• Ask colleagues to remind you about important events	• Change your seating and/or working positions
	• Incorporate movement in your day-to-day tasks

Sensory sensitivity	Sensation avoiding
• Choose a seating position which feels comfortable and a bit aside	• Prepare for the meeting as best you can. Sit in a corner, or at an end where there is no possibility of movement or action behind you. Reinforce the use of a structured, planned agenda. Run meetings early in the day rather than later
• Reduce glare on your PC screen	
• Turn down the ring volume on your phone; choose a softer, 'pleasant' ring tone for your cellphone	
	• Create clean and organized spaces (files, drawers, cupboards, shelves)
• Reduce clutter	• Use mute/dull colours
• Maintain good filing habits	• Turn your cellphone on mute/vibrate
• Use full-spectrum or natural lighting	• Move your seating away from air conditioner outflow, fan or open windows
• Use a blank screen saver on your PC	
• Use of quiet time and breaks is crucial	• Try to maintain a constant temperature within your working space
	• Reduce/remove auditory distractions (radio's etc.)
	• Use ear plugs or a head phone when noise levels get too much
	• Use of quiet time and breaks is crucial

These are some sensory ergonomics to assist you in establishing the idea of how, what and when to make changes that will assist with your performance. They are largely aimed at a general office space. Implementing the full extent of sensory ergonomics is only possible when done for a particular individual within a particular environment through a process of coaching and consulting. The possibilities are endless and obviously would differ from industry to industry and profile to profile.

Sensory trees and team dynamics

Revisit Chapter 4 for a full explanation of and discussion on relationship dynamics. The sensory tree can be used effectively with regard to team dynamics within an organization.

The two extremes of the sensory profile process are sensation seekers at the one extreme and sensation avoiders at the other extreme. Sensation seekers can be compared to the leaves of a tree; they are moving, change colour, get wind, sun, visits from birds, they fall off, regenerate and show growth in the tree. Sensation avoiders can be compared to the roots of a tree; they are deep down in the ground where it is cool, dark, calm and quiet. They anchor the tree and make sure the water is absorbed to ensure growth and stability.

It is interesting how this analogy works so well and rings so true for colleagues and/or team members in a work environment. These two profiles are direct opposites, their work style and approach are totally contradictory to one another. Sensation seekers need more input, facilitate change and growth and enjoy busy, novel environments. Sensation avoiders need less input; they avoid change and implement structure, routine and predictability. Although so different, both these approaches and working styles are crucial to sustaining any organization. It is the sensation seekers who often facilitate changes and growth in an organization while recruiting new clients and travelling. Sensation avoiders make sure that processes and procedures and the business core are maintained. They experience conflict as their core approach and needs are different, but both remain vital components for success.

Typical threshold individuals have neither sensitive nor seeking profile behaviours. They do not under- or over-respond to sensory input in their environments. My preliminary pilot studies using the profile indicate that only 18,5% of individuals tested fall within normal/typical thresholds. This type of profile can adapt easily to work with either avoiders or seekers. They are crucial in a work environment in view of the facilitating and balancing effect they have on others, employees and situations.

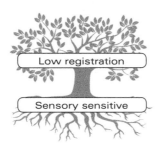

Low registrators are like the branches of a tree. They are on the high threshold spectrum but more passively inclined. They can be dreamers, yet conscientious, easily performing tasks and duties without experiencing disturbances from additional sensory input. Like branches they are steady and supply an important backbone. They make sure the food from the roots are carried through to the leaves. In work environments these profiles can easily switch off to maintain focus on the task at hand, but may miss important information, instructions or cues as a result of this.

Sensory sensitives are the surface roots of the tree. They are on the low threshold spectrum with sensitivity and awareness of the environment, but more passively inclined. They are acutely aware of their sensory environment but do not over-respond actively. They are therefore more tolerant of busy environments for longer periods of time than sensation avoiders. But they carry the same root tendencies; they prefer quietness, peace and calm, but do diligently and actively seek out these conditions. They are valuable because they are more in tune with others, processes and the environment. Individuals in this group are more likely to identify possible risks, errors and potential office disasters.

Considering these five different sensory profiles, with a large amount of possible mixes, different styles, different needs, different behaviours, there is bound to be conflict, especially between contrasting profiles. However, diversity of profiles within a work environment is crucial to sustaining operations, growth and change. Exploring the conflicts between profiles is crucial as it increases insight, facilitates acceptance and makes everyone realize that other people don't feel and experience the world the same way they do. Each profile has something unique to offer to the business process. I believe this is where the great power of sensory intelligence lies.

TEAM PROFILE CASE STUDY

I worked with a small financial investment company operating out of a townhouse in Hout Bay, Cape Town. The townhouse is situated on a seafront property. The area is quiet and tranquil, and most of the offices have a sea view. You can hear, see and smell the sea.

The CEO selected a small staff who did not enjoy working in big corporations. Apart from being in tune with his staff, he also has a relaxed and pro-active leadership style and regards a pleasant work environment as a vital requirement for optimum performance. The staff had an overall general productivity rating of 84%.

Their productivity statistics confirmed the fact that a perfect match between sensory profile and work environment was present. Working in this tranquil, seaside environment soothes the senses, enhances creativity and productivity. When I met with them they had been in operation for 18 months and managing R300 million per annum. Although they were productive and growing well, travelling and marketing were non-preferred tasks creating stress and overload. This is typical of low threshold profiles; they are good at and enjoy detail, structure and processes in a quiet environment. However, when required to handle marketing and travelling, more sensory input is inclined to lead to overload which often results in discomfort, irritability and stress.

Interventions were primarily focused on staff recruitment. The sensory intelligence process suggested that high threshold/sensation seeking individuals be recruited for the marketing, selling and travelling assignments. The company recruited four new staff members with sensation seeking traits, specifically for the marketing process. The company's turnover doubled within the following year.

The PEO model intervention

This model has been described extensively in Chapter 7 and will only be covered briefly. Performance in the workplace from a sensory intelligence perspective focuses on three main components:
- The person
- The work environment
- The occupation – job description and expectation

With optimal suitability between these three components, the individual will be performing at his or her peak.

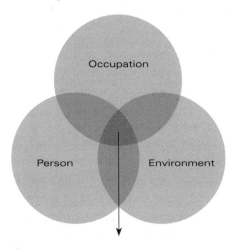

Occupational Performance

Using this model for intervention the following needs to be considered:

Person	Environment	Occupation
Sensory Profile Skills Education	Environmental analysis to determine sensory properties, structure and design, acoustics, lighting, space, chill/rest areas	Occupational analysis: task analysis and description, KPI – key performance indicators, KPA – key performance areas

Let's look at a practical example, based on a real case study, to explain the PEO model in action:

Person: Stacey*, 37-year old female	Environment: Loan department of small financial company	Occupation: Loan supervisor
Sensory profile: low threshold, active profile with significant sensitivity for the environment *Skills:* project administration, manage staff and information *Education:* post graduate diploma	*Environmental analysis:* Seated in middle of open-plan office, 30 square metres for 10 staff members; two phones on her desk, next to photocopy machine, seated under one of the three central air conditioner outflows in room. Area generally cluttered with three filing cabinets. Boxes, folders and files stacked against walls. Blue and brown colour schemes. No chill area except for a small kitchen area.	*Occupational analysis:* Phone and face-to-face contact with clients and colleagues, e-mail, faxing, copying and typing of documents, managing of loan-division staff, setting up meetings, processing and acceptance of applications.

Stacey's productivity was rated low by both her employer and herself. With the build-up of stress and expectation together with a feeling of being out of control, she was in tears about five times a day. During this stage she had to remove herself from the environment. Through the environmental analysis process it was identified that her seating arrangement within the open-plan office environment was contra-indicated by her sensory needs. Through a process of observation and documentation we established her arousal curve throughout a normal day. As discussed earlier, arousal refers to the alert state of the brain and is directly influenced by the type, intensity and amount of sensory input we receive at any given time during the course of a day. When we respond appropriately, we have a normal arousal level of the brain, creating optimal concentration. With too much sensory input and stress, sensory overload occurs. When sensory overload is prolonged, sensory shutdown occurs. Stacey's bursting into tears indicated a move from overload to shutdown; she had to leave her desk and office to pull herself together. Sensory overload is contra-indicated for performance and shutdown indicates zero performance. Before intervention, Stacey's pre-input arousal curve looked like this:

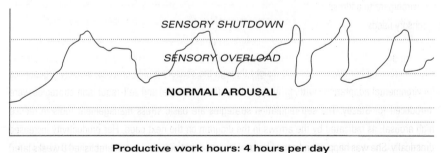

Productive work hours: 4 hours per day

Considering the PEO model, there was a poor goodness-of-fit between all constructs and Stacey's occupational performance reduced.

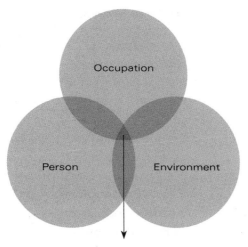

Reduced Occupational Performance

Intervention strategies were introduced as follows:

Person	Environment	Occupation
Introduce *self-regulation strategies* to reduce sensory overload and stress while at her desk. Taught *time management and organizational strategies.* Implemented *sensory diets* – activities to do in the home environment to address sensory needs.	*Sensory ergonomics* Moved her to the corner of the open-plan office, enlarged her space and used a divider. Moved her away from fax and photocopy machine and away from the air conditioner outflow. Turned down ringer volumes on phones. Turned her chair so that she was facing the window instead of the door.	Use of the quiet boardroom on Friday afternoons to catch up on backlog of work. Delegate certain low level tasks.

After increasing her awareness and insight through the sensory profile process, sensory ergonomics (environmental adaptations within the open-plan office structure) and self-regulation strategies were introduced for Stacey. The self-regulation strategies are basic stress management tools to reduce high arousal, as indicated by the arrows in the diagram on the next page. Her productivity increased drastically. She was happier and coped better. Her post-input arousal curve (established 8 weeks later) looked like this:

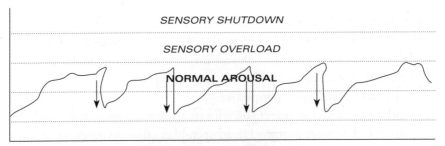

Productive work hours: 7 hours per day

Stacey's occupational performance was increased when a better fit was obtained between person, environment and occupation.

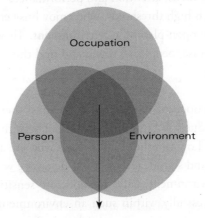

Greater Occupational Performance

Benefits were observed directly in the amount of productive work hours. The intervention had a personal gain for her but also for the team and the company.

Open-plan office environments

All environments have the potential to overload individuals. The extent of overload will be determined by the individual employee's neurological threshold and resultant sensitivity. Open-plan office environments, however, get special mention in view of their higher potential to impact on staff performance. The trend for the past 35 years in office design has been to move towards open-plan. It uses space more efficiently and is cost effective. It can be easily reconfigured and reduces construction cost. It also encourages teamwork, sharing of information, and is seen as motivational for employees. Nearly 75% of American and Canadian employees now work in open-plan office space as quoted by the Wall Street Journal online of 12 July 2002. However, employee satisfaction with an office environment also plays a role in its cost-effectiveness. If office conditions are poor, employees can become uncomfortable and dissatisfied, which may cancel out the expected savings.

From a *sensory intelligence* perspective:

- Individuals with low thresholds, who are sensitive to noise, vision and touch will be more distracted in an open-plan office environment. It will reduce their focus, attention and result in a significant drop in productivity. This is a potentially poor fit of the individual within the workspace.
- These individuals can benefit greatly from sensory ergonomics and self-regulation strategies to reduce sensory overload and stress, thereby increasing their focus, attention and performance.
- Individuals with high thresholds, who enjoy busy environments, will work well in an open-plan office environment. They will less likely be distracted by noise, people, or touch and find the sensory environment less distracting.

Sourcing staff for an open-plan office environment is therefore crucial and will establish higher production rates. The degrees of sensitivity responses should also be determined. Low threshold individuals who are at the bottom, lowest end of the extreme and significantly sensory defensive will most probably not cope in such an environment. Mild to moderate sensitivity can however be accommodated successfully within such an environment. Sensory ergonomics and self-regulation strategies are crucial and effective strategies. Successful "chill areas" is another important factor to consider. Any large open-plan office work environment should provide a quiet space for workers to rest, reduce their overload, self-calm and regulate.

Call centres

....

I devote a special section to call centres for two reasons: first, it is a special area of interest and my research specialization, and secondly it is one of the work environments with the biggest potential for sensory overload in the people working there.

A call centre or contact centre is a department or section of an organization specifically tasked with multi-media operations such as taking or making of calls or other forms of contact such as e-mail, Internet, video or fax. Call centres have procedures, supervision and technology aimed at supporting this task. In call centres, both inbound processes (mostly taking calls around customer queries) and/or outbound processes (making calls, usually to sell products) exist. Stringent surveillance and monitoring exists as calls are monitored for service quality. Employees' or agents' performance is measured accordingly. The call-centre industry is the fastest growing industry in South Africa with extensive capital investments from local government owing to its huge job-creation potential. Although companies identify the central role of human resources they seldom pay the necessary attention to training, retention and career development of their agents. The call-centre industry is known for being a busy, high-impact environment with high attrition rates. The general attrition rate as established by various studies is around 15% across the industry. This results in huge capital losses since training new agents is expensive.

General human resource structures and procedures often fail in the call-centre environment owing to the uniqueness of the setting. All work procedures of call-centre agents are monitored at all times which also adds to the stress and anxiety levels of agents in the field.

Considering the amount of sensory input that occurs in a call centre, it is a perfect situation to demonstrate the effect of sensory overload. There is a general busy-ness, activity, noise and movement in a call centre, matched by no other. It often feels like one is entering a beehive. For me it is the ultimate in sensory overload. Using sensory profiles and thresholds for the call centre industry is a valuable process in getting the most out of call centre agents. Based on the sensory profile I believe there is a particular profile that will cope best in the call-centre environment versus another that would not cope at all. By implementing this vital component I envisage a huge cost saving and bottom line benefit for the industry while creating a best-fit environment for individuals. It is a win-win situation!

Corporate case study titbits

Peter* is a 43 year old executive coach. He has a low threshold, active sensory profile with a tendency to avoid sensory input and a tendency to control his environment. Controlling the environment is very real, but very important for sensation avoiders. It is a coping strategy to increase predictability and while in control, the brain and body need to access less information through the senses. He gave up a very lucrative strategist career to become a coach. This change brought him more peace, job satisfaction and happiness. He also never works on a Friday and takes regular time off from his schedule. Naturally, Peter made significant contextual changes in his life when he changed his job. His current role fits his sensory needs far better, thus the improved quality of life. He runs regular leadership workshops and reported irritability and impatience with member attitudes. I recommended that he distribute his workshops equally across his schedule to avoid overbooking and make use of a facilitator for his workshops.

Evan* is a 42 year old MD of an international company. He has a very busy schedule and often travels for work. He has a sensation seeking profile, meaning he has high thresholds with an active tendency to create more sensory input in his environment. His profile process was very useful as it confirmed a positive goodness of fit with his current job description. He is successful at this job and enjoys the challenges. His concerns were mostly around time management, optimum stress management and saying yes to too much. Time management principles were stressed as well as the ability to be more assertive and self-care orientated to say no. Evan had to be coached specifically about identifying his stress zones as he often recognized them when too late. An accountability partner who knows him well was suggested to help him realize when he is reaching sensory overload and potential shutdown.

Monique* is a magazine journalist working for a media group. She has a significant sensory defensive profile and is negatively affected by her sensory environment to such an extent that she physically gets ill with sustained sensory overload and high stress periods without opportunity to self-regulate. She experiences significant sensory overload for auditory, visual and tactile input. As a result she finds her typical open-plan office environment daunting and tiring. She describes herself as a perfectionist, sensitive, short-tempered, critical and impatient. She gets tired and anxious quickly and hates to attend meetings. She finds commuting and travelling out of town exhausting.

Monique's sensory profile brought tremendous insight with regard to the implementation of a flexi-time schedule. She mostly works from home when on assignments and comes to the office a couple of days a week for meetings and consolidation. We also implemented commuting in off-peak traffic periods as much as possible, which made a huge difference to her stress levels. These shifts resulted in a marked increase in her performance and productivity. She also found that her relationships with colleagues improved and she won numerous awards and promotions for excellence. Luckily in Monique's case the flexi-schedule option was feasible and supported by her employer. Apart from these sensory ergonomics and adapting her work schedule, we also introduced self-regulation strategies to stay alert and reduce sensory overload. De-cluttering of workspace was another important component that had a contribution to visual overload. Monique is coping well, feeling much more in control, has dropped some of her self-obtained negative labels and is functioning optimally.

David* is a 32 year old agency administrator for a communications company. He is sensory defensive for auditory, touch, smell and visual input. He finds his sensory environment in the open-plan office environment extremely difficult to tolerate and reported that he is constantly distracted by his colleagues, TV and radio in the office and movement of his colleagues. A corner area with dividers was implemented for David but proved to be highly unsuccessful. He told me: "I can smell the people smoking on the balcony as their smoke is filtering through the air conditioners. You probably don't believe me?" I think David was relieved when I assured him that the one person who most certainly believed him was I. We used various techniques with earphones and earplugs to block out extraneous noise, which were not always practical, as David often had to make service telephone calls. We also implemented self-regulation strategies and sensory diets to control his stress levels outside of work. David struggled tremendously with organization and planning and we worked at various strategies to optimize time and organization. He also had collateral symptoms of an Attention Deficit Disorder. Despite our intervention strategies, David unfortunately still had an exceptionally high absenteeism rate. He was continuously seeing medical doctors and on anti-depressants on a regular basis. David's intervention process was part of a multidisciplinary approach with a psychiatrist and other therapists involved. He had low energy levels and found it difficult to sustain change and strategies that were implemented. He has a Bachelor degree in Industrial Psychology, but was in an administrative position. David just could not get in-sync with his environment and job expectations. He was under-performing and not working to his full potential. Eventually he was moved to a small closed-off office space, which he found, worked much better for him. Unfortunately, it created negative and jealous emotions from his colleagues and was reconsidered by his immediate head of department. David was a significant poor goodness-of-fit between his sensory profile, job description/occupational expectations and sensory environment. He eventually decided to give up his job and look for another position.

Jacques* is a 36 year old dentist. He is sensory defensive with significant low thresholds and sensitivity for auditory, touch, smell and visual information. He used to practice together with partners, but found it very difficult and as a result is now operating solo in his practice. He finds this much easier and manageable. He does not double up patients like other dentists because it makes him feel overloaded as he finds having to transition between two people continuously exhausting. What has become his trademark of working has also become a good selling strategy. Patients liked the idea that he was working with them and them alone without "sharing" him with another patient at the same time. His secretary/receptionist is like a stone barricade. She will not let you through either physically or telephonically without knowing all your credentials and background and will only then reluctantly transfer your call to him. She is an exceptionally good "filter" for Jacques, ensuring that he only needs to attend to important and urgent matters. Having to shift between tasks, multi-tasking and transitions are often difficult for individuals with sensory sensitivity. Jacques is a fanatic fly-fisherman and does regular exercise. He is using these activities to self-regulate/stress manage. The sensory profile did not facilitate change for Jacques, but confirmed his current working methods, preferences and irritations. He noted it a pity that he had to learn this through trial and error over the years, rather than having this as a tool at the start of his career. It assisted him however in future structuring, planning and choices. The emphasis and value of self-regulation and its wellness benefits were confirmed and were a driving force behind maintaining it.

Summary

How well are you suited to your current work position? Are you living your dream job? Do you enjoy your job, are motivated and actually look forward going to the office?

If yes, I challenge you to investigate your primary sensory needs and you will most likely find a positive correlation, thence your positive attitude, success and happiness. If no, I am convinced that on some level you will find a negative correlation between your sensory needs, your work environment and job description. Although people are not always in the fortunate position to change their situation, person-environment-job suitability should be the primary consideration on which selection of our work environment and job category is based. Beyond that, the value systems, social interactions, relationship dynamics, personalities, monetary compensations, energy and drive within a corporation – although not sensory related – then adds to our experience of job satisfaction. Based on my clinical experience, knowledge, client stories and assessments, I am convinced that sensory suitability and related goodness-of-fit are crucial and major considerations in optimizing human capital.

Index

M

movement 11, 23, 53, 61, 81, 137, 138, 140
   gravity 23
   living with 82
   motor patterns 23
   self-regulation through 140
   sensitive to 84
music 16, 137, 152 *See also* sound

N

noise *See also* sound
   background noise 15
   noise levels 15

O

occupation 42, 43, 44, 45, 121, 145
open-plan 178

P

PEO model 145, 175
personal space 18
planning 157

R

relationship 89, 93, 102, 145
   child 97
   dynamics 90, 95, 172
   parent 97, 102, 120
   partner 95, 104, 120
rest
   auditory system 17
   movement systems 25
   smell and taste systems 22
   tactile system 19
   visual system 14
root *See* sensation avoiding

self-care 145
stimulation 30
systems 29, 47
terminology 35
threshold 29, 149
tree 90, 172
typical threshold 91, 173
sensory defensive 29, 119, 126, 151
sensory intelligence (SIQ) 27, 148, 165, 168
  workplace 165
sensory seeking 126
sensory sensitive 38, 43, 92, 103, 104, 168, 170, 173
  See also sensory: low threshold
sight *See also* senses: visual
  living with 68
  self-regulation through 71, 141
  sensitive to 71
smell *See also* senses: chemical
  food 21
  high threshold 21
  living with 64
  low threshold 22
  self-regulation through 67
  sensitive to 67
sound 77, 152 *See also* senses: auditory
  living with 77
  self-regulation through 79, 142
  sensitive to 80
staff placement 169
stress 113, 152 *See also* self-regulation
surface root *See* sensory sensitive

T
....
taste *See also* senses: chemical
  food 21
  high threshold 21
  living with 64
  self-regulation through 67, 140
  sensitive to 67
therapy 151

References

Aaron, Elaine. N: (1999), *The highly sensitive person. How to thrive when the world overwhelms you.* Element / Harper Collins Publishers, New York, USA.

Allen, David: (2001), *Getting things done.* How to achieve stress-free productivity. Piatkus, London.

Brown, Catana: (2001), *What is the best environment for me? A sensory processing perspective.* The Haworth Press. Recovery and Wellness.

Brown, Catana E and Dunn, Winnie: (2002), *The Adolescent / Adult Sensory Profile.* The Psychological Corporation, San Antonio, Texas, USA.

Bundy, Anita; Lane, Shelley and Murray, Elizabeth: (2002), *Sensory integration theory and practice, second edition.* FA Davis Company, Philadelphia.

Campbell, Don: (1997), *The Mozart effect. Tapping the power of music to heal the body, strengthen the mind, and unlock the creative spirit.* Hodder and Stoughton, London.

Csikszentmihalyi, Mihaly: (1991), *Flow: The psychology of optimal experience.* Harper Perennial, New York.

Dunn, Winnie; Brown, Catana; and McGuigan, Ann: (July 1994), *The ecology of human performance: A framework for considering the effect of context.* The American Journal of Occupational Therapy, Volume 48, Number 7.

Dunn, Winnie: (November / December 2001), *The sensations of everyday life: empirical, theoretical, and pragmatic considerations.* The American Journal of Occupational Therapy, Volume 55, Number 6.

Dunn, Winnie: (2000), *Habit: What's the brain got to do with it?* The Occupational Therapy Journal of Research, Supplement 2000, Volume 20.

Eliot, Lise: (1999), *What's going on in there? How the brain and mind develop in the first five years of life.* Bantam Books, New York, USA.

Faure, Megan and Richardson, Anne: (2002), *Baby sense. Understanding your baby's sensory world – the key to a contented child.* Metz Press, Cape Town, South Africa.

Heller, Sharon: (2002), *Too loud, too bright, too fast, too tight: What to do if you are sensory defensive in an over stimulating world.* Harper Collins, New York, USA.

Pfeiffer, Beth and Kinnealey, Moya: (2003), *Treatment of sensory defensiveness in adults.* Occupational Therapy International, Volume 10 Number 3.

Ratey, Johan: (2001), *A user's guide to the brain.* Little, Brown and Company, London.

Roley, S; Blanche, Erna and Schaaf, Roseann: (2001), *Understanding the nature of sensory integration with diverse populations.* Therapy Skills Builders, USA.

Strong, Susan; Rigby, Patty; Stewart, Debra; Law, Mary; Letts, Lori and
Cooper Barbara: (June 1999), *Application of the person-environment-
occupation model: A practical tool.* Canadian Journal of Occupational
Therapy, Volume 66, Issue 3.

Tortora, Gerard. J and Grabowski, Sandra Reynolds: (1996), *Principles of
anatomy and physiology, Eighth edition.* Harper Collins College Publishers,
New York, USA.

Viljoen, Henning; van Staden, Fred; Grieve, Kate; and van Deventer, Vasi:
(1987, 1988, 1992, 1993), *Environmental psychology, An Introduction.*
Lexicon Publishers, Johannesburg, South Africa.

Williams, M.S and Shellenberger, S: (1994), *How does your engine run?
A leader's guide to the alert program for self-regulation.* Therapyworks,
New Mexico, USA.

Zuckerman, Marvin: (1994), *Behavioural expressions and bio-social bases of
sensation seeking.* Cambridge University Press, New York, USA.

Links:

The Adolescent/Adult Sensory profile
   www.sensoryprofile.com
The Alert program: Shelley Shellenberger and Mary Sue Williams
   www.alertprogram.com
Morton, Jill: Colour Voodoo for the Office
   www.colorvoodoo.com
Martin Lindstrom: Sensory branding
   www.brandsense.com
Megan Faure: Sensory integration for babies
   www.babysense.com
Sensory integration for children
   www.SPDnetwork.com
Elaine Aron: The highly sensitive person
   www.hsperson.com
About the Alfred Tomatis method
   www.tomatis.com
About auditory integration training
   www.auditoryintegration.net
   www.mind-works.co.za
About full spectrum lighting
   www.fullspectrumsolutions.com
   www.naturallighting.com